CW01507688

Daring Destiny
The metamorphosis of
Omo-oniresi

Oludare Anuodo

Published by New Generation Publishing in 2025

Copyright © Oludare Anuodo

First Edition

The author asserts the moral right under the Copyright, Designs and Patents Act 1988 to be identified as the author of this work.

All Rights reserved. No part of this publication may be reproduced, stored in a retrieval system or transmitted, in any form or by any means without the prior consent of the author, nor be otherwise circulated in any form of binding or cover other than that which it is published and without a similar condition being imposed on the subsequent purchaser.

ISBN 978-1-83563-621-3

www.newgeneration-publishing.com
New Generation Publishing

To Obafemi, Ooreofe and Ajibike

In Memory of Gbenga Afolabi Anuodo
(1963-2004)

Table of Contents

PREFACE

Life, a tapestry woven with threads of joy and sorrow, is a journey of constant evolution. This autobiography is my humble attempt to encapsulate this intricate odyssey, to share the poignant moments that have defined my existence, shaped my character, and transformed me into the individual I am today. Through these pages, I offer a candid glimpse into the labyrinth of my world, an exploration of my past, a profound understanding of my present, and a vision for a brighter future that beckons on the horizon.

This endeavor has been a deeply personal and introspective journey, demanding that I delve into the recesses of my memory, unearthing both cherished recollections and the poignant echoes of pain. It has been an opportunity for reflection, a time to contemplate the lessons learned, both profound and subtle, and to celebrate the triumphs, both grand and minute, that have punctuated my life. This narrative is a testament to self-discovery, a chronicle of doggedness, a celebration of the fighting spirit, a beacon of resilience, and an ode to the enduring capacity for human growth.

My sincere hope is that by sharing my story, I may offer a beacon of inspiration to others, a source of solace in their own journeys, and a gentle reminder that they are not alone in their struggles and triumphs. Perhaps, in the resonance of my narrative, others will find the courage to embark upon their own literary journeys, to share their own unique stories with the world.

Hailing from humble beginnings as the son of a junior university staff member, I could scarcely have envisioned the trajectory my life would take. Raised in a crucible of adversity, I faced challenges that would have deterred many. Yet, through unwavering determination and the grace of divine providence, I have defied expectations, earning a doctoral degree and forging a career in academia, both within the vibrant intellectual landscape of Nigeria and within the hallowed halls of British education.

My academic pursuits have yielded a measure of success, with my contributions recognized and cited by scholars worldwide. While I do not claim to possess exceptional brilliance, I am deeply grateful for the opportunities that have unfolded before me. Indeed, it is through the grace of God that I have surpassed even my own wildest dreams.

As a child, I harbored a yearning for flight, a desire to soar above the limitations of my circumstances. This youthful aspiration has found unexpected fulfillment, as I have journeyed across continents, from the heart of Africa to the far reaches of Asia, America, and Europe.

My journey began inauspiciously, a seven-year-old boy venturing onto the streets to hawk rice and stew to support my family. This early encounter with adversity forged an indomitable spirit, equipping me to navigate the challenges that lay ahead. From the vibrant academic landscape of Nigerian universities, where I nurtured the minds of eager undergraduates and postgraduate students, my path led me to the classrooms of the United Kingdom, where I imparted knowledge to high school and college students. Now, I find myself serving within the National Health Service NHS, continuing to contribute to the well-being of my community. My life's journey stands as a testament to the indomitable human spirit, a narrative of perseverance triumphing over adversity.

From the earliest stages of my life, a profound aspiration has taken root within me: to break the cycle of poverty that has plagued generations of my family. This ambition was deeply ingrained, nurtured by the wisdom of my father, who often invoked the Yoruba proverb, *"Iran meta ki i toshi"* – "poverty should not persist for three generations." Though my grandfather, Benjamin Anuodo, passed away in 1972, three years before my birth, I understood from the echoes of family history that he, like my father, had lived a life of modest means.

As a child, I vowed to sever the chains of poverty that had bound my family for generations. Through the grace of God and the unwavering support of those around me, I have, to a degree, succeeded in breaking those chains. Now, I carry the torch, instilling in my children, Ooreofe and Obafemi, an unshakeable belief in their ability to achieve greatness. I fervently hope that they will carry this legacy forward, breaking free from the shackles of limitation and inspiring future generations to reach for the stars, soaring to heights unimaginable by their ancestors.

My life's narrative would have undoubtedly unfolded differently were it not for the unwavering support of my elder brother, Tayo. From our earliest days, he recognized not merely a sibling, but a project, a nascent potential to be nurtured and cultivated. He stepped into the void left by the untimely demise of our elder brother, Gbenga, assuming the mantle of sole provider and financier.

During the tumultuous economic climate that gripped our nation, Tayo stood as a steadfast pillar of support. His acts of kindness, often performed discreetly, extended to my wife, offering crucial financial assistance during our most challenging times. When illness threatened to extinguish my spirit, it was his unwavering determination that kept my flame alive. For his unwavering support and unwavering belief in me, I am eternally grateful.

Despite his demanding schedule, Tayo graciously dedicated his time to the editing and refinement of this work. His meticulous eye for detail and his profound understanding of the narrative allowed him to seamlessly fill in the gaps, elevating the manuscript to new heights. His personal connection to the story, having witnessed firsthand the challenges I faced, imbued his contributions with a profound empathy and authenticity. As we navigated the editing process, tears often flowed freely, a shared catharsis that deepened the bond between us. Tayo candidly admitted that until he delved into the manuscript, he had not fully comprehended the depth of adversity I had endured. His unwavering encouragement and swift responses to my queries were instrumental in propelling the story to completion.

The profound impact of marriage on a man's life is a well-documented phenomenon. In my own experience, I can attest to its transformative power. My wife, Ajibike, has been my steadfast companion, my guiding star. Without her unwavering encouragement and unwavering support, this literary endeavor would have remained but a fleeting dream. Her gentle spirit has tempered my fiery nature, creating a harmonious balance. I am eternally grateful to the divine for bestowing upon me such a remarkable partner, a true helper of my destiny.

To the constellation of educators who have illuminated my path, and to all those who have left an indelible mark on my journey, I express my sincerest gratitude. Your guidance, your wisdom, and your unwavering belief in my potential have shaped the person I am today.

CHAPTER ONE
MY EARLY CHILDHOOD

The year was 1975, in the month of July, peak of the rainy season, a time when the skies would often weep torrents of rain, flooding the streets and saturating the air with a humid, oppressive heat. The city was awash in a kaleidoscope of green, as lush vegetation thrived in the abundant rainfall. Against this backdrop of natural beauty and seasonal intensity, a new life was poised to emerge.

July 11th, at the modest Health Centre Okesha Ado Ekiti, a miracle unfolded. A mid age woman, her body heavy with the weight of a new life, lay on a simple hospital bed, her eyes filled with anticipation and a touch of fear. As the hours passed, the tension in the room grew palpable. The doctors and nurses, their faces etched with concern, watched over the expectant mother, their hearts pounding in unison with hers.

Rachael Aboja, a woman of strength and resilience, was about to welcome her fifth child into the world. Rachael's family was a tapestry woven with love and anticipation. Her eldest, Gbenga, a twelve-year-old first year boy at Ado Grammar School, was eager to embrace the role of a big brother. Tayo, the youngest, a brilliant three-year-old bundle of energy, yearned for a playmate. The entire household was abuzz with excitement, each member harbouring their own secret desires for the new-born.

In those days, the modern marvel of ultrasound was not yet to be popular or within the reach of the poor. The expectant parents could only speculate about the gender of their unborn child. Afolabi Michael, Rachael's husband, harboured a deep-seated yearning for a son. He envisioned a male child who would join the two on the ground to carry on the family name and traditions. Rachael, on the other hand, was more concerned with the well-being of her child. Based on her previous experiences, she was convinced that she was carrying a baby girl.

Tayo, with his innocent heart, yearned for a brother to share his adventures. He would often be found whispering secrets to his mother's pregnant belly, imagining the day when his new sibling would join him in their playful escapades. Yemisi, the elder of the two girls, and Toyin were just waiting for a baby that they could back with wrappers and plait the hair. They cared less about the gender.

As the day of Rachael's delivery approached, the family prepared with a mix of anticipation and trepidation. Rachael's bag was packed with a carefully curated selection of baby clothes, both for male and female, reflecting the uncertainty surrounding the baby's gender.

On Friday, 11th of July, 1975 at about half past ten in the morning, Rachael was ushered into the delivery room, her husband by her side. The birthing process was a relatively smooth one, a testament to her strength and resilience. As she knelt down, a surge of energy propelled her forward, and with one push, a huge bundle of joy emerged weighing above four kilograms with a noticeable big head. This is indeed a big miracle, the room erupted in cheers as a baby boy was placed into Rachael's arms. The time was 11:00 AM, a moment that would forever be etched in the family's memory. Afolabi my father was so happy for the arrival of his third boy, a son he has so much looked forward to receiving. For him, it was a case of "I knew it". Eight days later, the community gathered to celebrate the new-born's christening. The ceremony took place at number 8 Anuodo Street, Okeila, Ado Ekiti, during the reign of Oba Daniel Anirare Aladesanmi II, the revered Ewi of Ado Ekiti.

Afolabi Michael, overcome with joy, wasted no time in naming his son *Oluwadamilare,* a name that translated to "God has vindicated me." Rachael, though surprised by the gender, accepted God's will and bestowed upon her son the name *Ifeoluwa,* meaning "it is the God's will." Thus, the story of *Oluwadamilare* began, a tale woven with love, anticipation, and the divine intervention that has shaped his destiny. As I grew older, I have come to appreciate the significance of my name, a reminder of my parents' hopes and dreams, and the miraculous circumstances of my birth.

In the year 1980, I embarked on my academic odyssey, joining my elder brother, Tayo, at Mary Mount Primary School in Oke-Ila, Ado Ekiti. Back then, the prerequisites for entering primary school were quite straightforward: one had to be six years of age, possess knowledge of their full name, and be able to state their age. The most challenging criterion, however, involved stretching one's arm over one's head, beginning from the right ear, and ensuring it reached the left ear.

Despite being only five years old, I possessed the physical stature of an eight-year-old and the intellectual acumen of a twelve-year-old. As a result, meeting these criteria was a breeze for me, allowing me to secure admission into primary school at the tender age of five. My initial days at school were etched into my memory. Tayo, already a Primary Three pupil, was held in high esteem by both teachers and students. The entire school rejoiced at my arrival.

My brother was renowned for his academic prowess, consistently garnering all the accolades for winning all the prizes at the end-of-term prize-giving ceremonies. He was also celebrated for his exceptional talent in the school's theatre group. The entire school eagerly anticipated his performances, and his masterful delivery of his roles invariably elicited thunderous applause.

My early years in Ado Ekiti were a tale of resilience and faith lazed with threads of hardship and hope. Despite our modest humbled circumstances, we carried ourselves with a sense of pride and unwavering joy. Our father, Afolabi, worked diligently as a junior staff member at the University of Ife, first as a staff of Sanitary and Maintenance unit, then worked briefly as a laundry attendant at the university Halls of Residence before he moved to the Security Unit, where he worked as a Porter in the Halls of Residence namely; Angola Hall, Fajuyi Hall, Awolowo Hall and Postgraduate Hall where he retired at the age of 60 years.

My eldest brother, Gbenga, initially followed in my father's footsteps, after he finished Grammar School joined the University of Ife as an Administrative officer in the Senate Building. Aunty Sade Osiberu who was a Principal Registrar of the University as at the time assisted him.   However, Gbenga's academic aspirations led him to secure a coveted place at the prestigious University of Ife in 1984. He became the first of his generation to achieve such feat. He also became a reference point to all family to encourage their own children.

The remaining six of us remained at Ado Ekiti under the watchful care of our mother, a dedicated caterer. Each morning, from Monday to Saturday, she would rise before dawn to prepare sumptuous meals for those who were unable to cook at home. By 6 a.m., her culinary creations were ready to be distributed. With remarkable strength, she would carry a large pan of steaming rice and seasoned stew on her head to her bustling selling point near our family residence at Okeila.

Around 11 a.m., she would embark on another culinary journey, delivering her delectable dishes to a government-operated primary school, Local Authority School, Aafin Oba, Ado Ekiti. Despite my mother's hard work, the responsibilities on her, the number of mouths she has to feed turned her to becoming a debtor to many sellers of raw food stuffs in the market. I can never forget the recurring humiliations she endured. Vendors would often visit our home, demanding payment for outstanding debts. Their verbal assaults were cruel and disheartening. As a child, I wondered why my mother couldn't simply settle these debts.

However, as I matured, I realized her unwavering commitment to providing for our family of seven. She would often send food to our father in Ile-Ife, even during our most challenging times. I recall witnessing her tears of frustration and embarrassment, which fuelled my determination to one day alleviate her financial burdens and bail her out of the debt mystery.

CHILD LABOUR VERSUS FAMILY LOVE

In contemporary discourse, the notion of child labour often elicits amusement among those who perceive it as a Western ideological imposition, incompatible with traditional

African societal norms. From generations past to the present, children have been integral participants in their families' economic activities. Large families were once considered a valuable asset, providing a readily available workforce to contribute to agricultural endeavours, trade, or commerce.

The moment a child grasps the concept of monetary value, they are poised to contribute to the family's commercial endeavors. In my case, this initiation occurred between the ages of seven and eight, when I embarked on the journey of peddling rice and stew on behalf of my mother. As a young child, I eagerly anticipated the day when I would be old enough to participate in this cherished family tradition.

Each morning, before the school bell rang, I would prepare for my daily task. Between the hours of seven and eight in the morning, cooked rice would be meticulously wrapped in large leafs called '*ewe-iran*' or coco-yam leafs, ensuring equal portions. These parcels would then be artfully arranged around a metal tray, with a small bowl of seasoned stew nestled in the center. The dimensions of the food trays we carried were typically dictated by the physical capacity of the bearer. This daily routine, undertaken before our morning meal and school attendance, was a source of communal joy.

A particularly poignant memory from this period emerged during the tumultuous '*Weti e*' crisis of south-western Nigeria in 1983. In our home state of Ondo, a fierce political battle unfolded between incumbent Governor

Michael Adekunle Ajasin of the United Peoples Party (UPN) and his former deputy, Akinwole Michael Omoboriowo, who had defected to the National Party of Nigeria (NPN) to challenge his ex-boss. Despite initially being declared the victor, Omoboriowo's triumph was contested and subsequently overturned by a court of appeal before he could assume office. This legal reversal ignited a wave of violence across the state.

On that fateful August morning, my siblings and I ventured out early to hawk rice and stew. As tensions escalated, our mother's anxiety grew as my elder siblings returned home, but I remained unaccounted for. The streets were engulfed in chaos as supporters of the two rival parties engaged in destructive acts, torching houses and vehicles, and vandalizing property. Seeking refuge, I concealed my nearly depleted tray of rice within a thicket of bushes and joined a group of UPN supporters, finding juvenile amusement in their chants, war songs, and acts of vandalism. After several hours, I retraced my steps and returned to my family, who were overjoyed to see me safe.

Though we were involved in activities that might today be classified as child labour, at the time, we did not perceive it as exploitation by our parents. Instead, we viewed it as a way to contribute to our family's well-being, supporting our parents' arduous efforts to provide for us.

MY MOTHER'S FAITH AND DEVOTION

My mother was a devout Christian, whose faith was the cornerstone of her life. She was a woman of unwavering prayer, and I often found her kneeling in fervent supplication in the dead of night. In those days, corporal punishment was a common disciplinary tactic, but my mother preferred a gentler approach. Her primary form of punishment was to have us kneel and pray.

If you confided in her about feeling unwell, she would prescribe a unique prayer as a remedy: "*Jesu Deje re bomi, feje re we mi*," which translates to "I am covered by the blood of Jesus, I am bathed in the blood of Jesus." This prayer could be recited for hours, sometimes even extending into sleep.

Despite our economic hardships, we experienced an abundance of joy and love within our family. Our mother never complained or spoke negatively about our father. She was a shining example of a noble woman, always praying for our future. She generously shared her meals with the less fortunate in our neighbourhood, including the motherless and the widowed. Although she lacked formal education, my mother was a fluent reader of the Yoruba Bible. She was the eldest child of Eyemogbolare, a renowned kolanut seller. Her only sibling, Ogamotayo, a successful commercial driver, had unfortunately abandoned her in times of need, displaying a callous disregard for her well-being.

In the year 1983, Nigeria found itself grappling with a severe economic downturn. The nation's economy became fragile coupled with rampant corruption, this necessitated a drastic intervention. The military, seizing the opportunity, ousted the democratically elected government of Alhaji Shehu Shagari. General Muhammadu Buhari ascended to power as the head of state, vowing to restore order and integrity to the nation. Initially, the military regime seemed poised to make a positive impact. The introduction of the War against Indiscipline (WAI) aimed to curb corruption and instil discipline within society. However, the initial optimism soon waned as the economic crisis deepened.

RELOCATION TO ILE IFE

Families struggled to put food on the table, and the burden on my parents became increasingly heavy. Amidst this turmoil, a difficult decision was made: three of us children would join my father and brother in Ile-Ife. The criteria for selecting the three children remain a mystery to me even till today. However, the decision was final: my eldest sister, Yemisi, my younger brother, Femi, and I were chosen to leave the familiar comforts of Ado Ekiti.

Relocating to Ile-Ife was akin to stepping into a different world. It was as if we had been transported from a quaint village to the bustling metropolis of the United States. The contrast between our humble abode in Ado Ekiti and the modern comforts of Ile-Ife was stark. Our father's residence at No 54B Oroona Street, Modakekc Ile-Ife (Ile Baba Ijebu) was a-story building equipped with flush toilets, a far cry from the rudimentary latrines we had grown accustomed to in Ado Ekiti.

The transition to Ile-Ife was not without its challenges. We were thrust into a new environment, surrounded by unfamiliar faces and circumstances. However, we were determined to adapt and make the best of our new lives. Sister Yemisi General Schools Certificate Examination results was not so good. She was enrolled into Modakeke High School through the help of Mrs Olomola. Femi and I were enrolled into Primary 1 and 4 at Christ Apostolic Church Primary School, Ondo Road.

Our father and elder brother provided invaluable support and guidance. They helped us acclimate to the new lifestyle, introduced us to the local community, and ensured that our educational needs were met. The university's vibrant atmosphere and intellectual stimulation provided a stark contrast to the limited opportunities available in Ado Ekiti. Despite the economic hardships that plagued Nigeria at the time, we found solace in the support and love of our family. My parents, despite their own struggles, remained steadfast in their commitment to providing for us. They instilled in us the importance of education and perseverance, even in the face of adversity.

As we settled into our new life in Ile-Ife, we began to explore the city and its surroundings. The transition to Ile-Ife was a significant turning point in our lives. It exposed us to new experiences, broadened our horizons, and prepared us for the challenges that lay ahead. The memories of that time remain etched in my mind, a testament to the resilience and adaptability of the human spirit. My stay in Ile-Ife was unfortunately short-lived. Having completed primary school, I gained admission to the prestigious Seven Day Adventist Grammar School in Ile-Ife. However, fate had other plans.

In December 1986, my brother Femi and I embarked on a journey with our father's cousin, Pastor Eiyebiokin, to Ado Ekiti to celebrate Christmas and New Year with our mother and other siblings. Our initial plan was to return to Ile-Ife in January to resume our studies. However, the unrelenting economic hardships faced by my parents forced them to make a difficult decision. They concluded that it would be in our best interest for either my elder brother, Tayo, or me to live with my maternal uncle, Mr. Segun Ola. Once again, I found myself chosen to embark on a new adventure.

THE EMBRACE OF A NEW FAMILY

Mr. Segun Ola and his young family resided in Akure, the capital city of Ondo State. At the time, He had four children; three boys and a girl. His eldest Olajumoke, nine years old.

Adedamola the oldest of the three boys was seven years old, then Adeola and Adegboyega. Both Mr. Ola and his wife held prominent positions in the Ondo State government civil service. His wife served as the chief caterer at the governor's residence, while he was a respected director in one of the state ministries. They were in need of a young boy to assist with household chores and care for their children while they were at work. This arrangement would alleviate the financial burden on my parents, as I would essentially become their responsibility.

My uncle's household welcomed me with an openhearted warmth that belied my recent arrival. The children, in particular, embraced me as if I were a long-lost sibling, their affection genuine and immediate. Mrs. Ademade Ola, my uncle's wife, exuded a gracious hospitality, treating me with the same tenderness she bestowed upon her own children. I addressed her as "Mummy," and my uncle as "Daddy," these titles echoing the profound sense of belonging that began to bloom within me. This home, I realized, had been awaiting my arrival.

It was here that I first tasted margarine (Blue Band). I had, of course, heard whispers of butter, a coveted indulgence reserved for the affluent children, the taste though proved a stark contrast to my imagination. I mimicked my new "brothers", spreading the unfamiliar substance upon bread, only to be met with a disconcerting flavor, a curious blend of salt and oil, a sensation both foreign and unsatisfying.

In this house of plenty, where sustenance flowed freely and appetites were indulged without restraint, a poignant dissonance resonated within me. Witnessing the discarded remnants of meals, a lavish abundance that stood in stark contrast to the precarious food dearth of my family back in Ile-Ife, would often elicit a silent, tearful lament.

Each evening, after diligently completing my household chores and school homework, I would retreat to the seclusion of the backyard. Perched upon a concrete slab over a soak-away, I would gaze longingly at the vast canvas of the night sky, my thoughts yearning for the connection with my younger brothers, Femi and Tosin, who remained far away in Ile-Ife. These nocturnal vigils were often punctuated by silent tears, a melancholic release of the profound longing that gnawed at my heart, a longing concealed from the watchful eyes of my uncle's family.

Despite the material comforts and the genuine affection that surrounded me, a profound sense of displacement lingered. I felt like a displaced soul, a leaf torn from its branch, adrift in a sea of unfamiliar circumstances. Though nourished and cherished, my heart yearned for the familiar embrace of my impoverished family, for the unbreakable bond shared with my siblings.

My time in Akure revealed a previously unknown side of my life. My uncle, a vibrant and charismatic man, possessed a deep appreciation for life's pleasures. He was an exemplary civil servant, tall, fair in skin and handsome, admired by women of all ages. My uncle was an active member of several social clubs, particularly Club 20. His daily routine involved leaving home for work in the morning around 7am, returning around 5 p.m., changing into casual attire, enjoying sumptuous dinner, and then heading to his club house. He would typically return home around 9:30 p.m., relax in the living room or on the balcony with a chilled bottle of Star beer and a few cigarettes before retiring to bed.

Living with my uncle exposed me to a different lifestyle. Despite the initial challenges of adjusting to a new environment, I gradually settled into my new home. I formed bonds with my cousins and became familiar with the neighbourhood. The experience also helped me develop a sense of independence and self-reliance.

However, this era, ushered me into a markedly distinct milieu, a stark contrast to the environment I had hitherto inhabited within the confines of my parents' household. Here, I encountered a pervasive sense of liberty, permeating every facet of existence. Mornings would witness my departure for school, yet my return was entirely at my discretion, provided I made it home before the conclusion of the civil servants' workday. No one scrutinized my academic progress or the completion of assigned homework. As long as I fulfilled my domestic responsibilities, I was afforded a remarkable degree of autonomy. This unfettered freedom, far from cultivating the blossoming of my potential, inadvertently exerted a pernicious influence upon my character

A DESCENT INTO DARKNESS

My luck held once more as I secured admission to Oyemekun Grammar School, Akure. Renowned for its academic excellence, OGSA was considered the pinnacle of education not only in Akure but throughout the entire state. However, beneath its pristine facade lurked a darker side, as the school was also notorious for fostering truancy and delinquent behaviour among its students.

Unfortunately, my newfound freedom led me down a perilous path. After my first year, I abandoned my academic pursuits and succumbed to the negative influences that permeated the school. I became entangled with a group of troublemakers, skipping classes at will and engaging in frequent brawls. I abandoned my studies altogether, preferring the thrill of amateur boxing and the intoxicating allure of cigarettes and marijuana.

My uncle and aunt were oblivious to my descent into darkness. They assumed that I was diligently attending school, while I was indulging in illicit activities. One fateful day, while attempting to escape school through a narrow footpath that bordered St. Peter's Unity School, I was caught by the Vice Principal, Mr. Oluyombo (not a real name). He administered a severe flogging, igniting a smouldering ember of resentment within me. Determined to exact revenge, I plotted to ambush Mr. Oluyombo on his usual route home. Armed with a catapult and a carefully chosen stone, I waited patiently for my opportunity. When the moment arrived, I released the stone, striking him squarely on the head. The impact caused a deep wound, and blood gushed from his scalp.

The school administration could no longer tolerate my rebellious behaviour. I was summoned to the principal's office and issued an expulsion order. This incident served as a wake-up call, a harsh reality that shattered the illusions I had been clinging to. Tears streamed down my face as I realized the depth of my shame. I had not only betrayed myself but also my family, and the weight of their disappointment was unbearable.

I returned home, concealing my expulsion from my uncle. At night, alone in my room, I wept uncontrollably, consumed by guilt and remorse. I continued to deceive everyone including myself unfortunately, collecting my school fees and squandering them on frivolous pursuits. When the end of the academic session approached, I fabricated a fake result to avoid detection. As the days turned into weeks and months, the consequences of my actions became increasingly apparent. My future was in jeopardy, and I had become a disillusioned and aimless individual. Only divine intervention could save me from the abyss into which I had fallen.

One fateful day, one of my uncles, Mr Sunday Ola, a secondary school teacher at Odigbo High School, Odigbo, visited our home at Akure. He requested my end of session results, and I presented him with the forged document. However, his keen eye spotted a glaring grammatical error in the principal's comment, exposing my deception. Instead of "keep it up", I unknowingly wrote "keep it off"!

The following Monday, my uncle accompanied me to Oyemekun Grammar School, where my shame was laid bare. The school authorities revealed my expulsion, and my uncle was mortified. I knew that I would face severe consequences upon my return home. Fear consumed me, and I made a desperate decision: to run away. That night, I sneaked out of my room while my family was gathered in the living room. I packed my belongings and fled into the darkness, seeking refuge in an unfinished building in a dangerous neighbourhood.

In the dead of night, around one o'clock, I lay awake in my dark room, my mind racing with a whirlwind of thoughts. Suddenly, I heard a conversation emerging from the darkness, a chilling plot to rob a nearby compound. Terror seized me, and I held my breath, paralyzed by fear that they might suspect someone was listening to their nefarious plans. The silence was suffocating, so intense that even a pin drop would have shattered the fragile tranquillity.

After a few tense minutes, they vanished, and the silence was pierced by the deafening sound of gunshots. The night stretched out before me, filled with dread and the constant threat of danger. The next morning, I dressed hastily, concealing my bag of belongings. I made a resolute decision: I would not return to that perilous building, no matter what. How could I explain myself if the police arrived to arrest armed robbers, and I was found in their vicinity? No one would believe my innocence, given my past transgressions.

Desperate for a safe haven, I sought advice from Galome, a member of my gang. He suggested that I seek refuge in a church with a large compound, a place where I could find sanctuary. His advice seemed sound, and I realized that what I needed most at that moment was prayer, for my situation was beyond human redemption, and I yearned for divine intervention. Around four o'clock in the afternoon, I returned to the dreaded building to retrieve my belongings. To my dismay, my bag had been taken, leaving me with only the clothes I was wearing. Heartbroken but undeterred, I continued my search for a church to provide shelter.

As I wandered through the streets, the memory of Christ Apostolic Church Olorunkosheunti of Prophet Dr. T. O. Obadare came to mind. In those days, the church compound was a bustling hub of activity, attracting thousands of people from all over the world seeking miracles. I decided that this was the place I needed to be. I was familiar with the church, as we had once lived in a building that shared a fence with it. Upon arriving at WOSEM, as the church ground was called, I joined the long queue of worshippers awaiting dinner. I devoured the food with a voracious appetite, having gone nearly 72 hours without a proper meal.

After dinner, I joined the multitude of worshippers in prayer, I sought divine forgiveness and restoration. I poured out my heart, confessing the terrible sins I had committed against God. I knew that if He would forgive me, I could face the consequences of my actions before my uncle and parents. That night, I slept peacefully for the first time in three days, my slumber undisturbed by fear or anxiety.

The following morning, a family friend of my uncle spotted me at the miracle ground, looking dishevelled and distraught. News of my escapades had reached Ado Ekiti and Ileife. My father dispatched my eldest brother, Gbenga, to travel to Akure to see me. When he arrived at my uncle's house, he was told that I had run away from home and that the matter had been reported to Police.

The next day, members of my family came to find me, discovering me in the same place where I had been sleeping. I was a shadow of my former self, looking dusty, unkempt, and almost unrecognizable. They took me home. At home, I braced myself for the inevitable consequences of my actions. I knew I deserved whatever punishment awaited me, and I was prepared to face the repercussions of my delinquent behaviour.

My brother convened a meeting with my uncle, who was still reeling from the shock of my shameful actions. He felt betrayed, having invested in my education, provided for my needs, and paid my school fees. Yet, I had repaid his kindness with truancy and delinquency, ultimately leading to my expulsion.

Instead of resorting to physical punishment, they merely stared at me, their eyes filled with a mixture of disappointment and disgust, as if I were a leper. My uncle was unwilling to be involved in the search for a new school. He informed my brother that he would have sent me away from his house to prevent me from becoming a negative influence on his own children.

Gbenga, my eldest brother, contacted my father at IleIfe by phone, he suggested that he take me to see his childhood friend, Professor Ishola Olomola, who happened to be the Commissioner of Education in Ondo State at the time. My brother agreed, and he explained my situation to the commissioner. At the Commissioner's Lodge in Alagbaka Akure, my brother left me and returned to Ileife, while I remained under the care of the Commissioner.

REDEMPTION AND TRIUMPH: A SECOND CHANCE

Professor Olomola was a stern and disciplined individual, refusing to use his position as Commissioner of Education to seek personal favours from any school principal in Akure. After spending four days in his house, he informed me that I would be accompanying him to his office at the Governor's office the following day. He mentioned that he would be meeting with several school principals from Akure and planned to discuss my case with them, hoping to find a school willing to accept me.

I dressed neatly and waited patiently for a long time at the reception area. Eventually, the secretary summoned me to the commissioner's office. Inside, I met a middle-aged man with a stern expression, Mr. E. R. A. Babalola, the Principal of Aquinas College Akure. I entered the office and stood respectfully, gazing at the ceiling. In his deep, authoritative voice, Mr. Babalola asked me if I was ready to return to school. I replied affirmatively, eager to start a new chapter in my life. He assured me that he could handle me in his school and instructed me to report for enrolment the following Monday.

On Monday, I arrived at Aquinas College and headed straight Away to the principal's office, anticipating him to assign me a class. However, to my disappointment, the principal informed me that my case had been discussed at the staff meeting. They had decided to place me in Junior Secondary School Two (JSS 2'6), much to my dismay.

My former classmates at Oyemekun Grammar School were already in Senior Secondary School One (SS1). The explanation they provided was that I could not be placed in SS1 because I had not completed the JSS3 Examinations, and they could not enrol me in JSS3 as the registration for Junior WAEC had already closed. It was then that I realized the full extent of my punishment. My involvement in gangsterism and thuggery had cost me two precious years of my early life. Life had not dealt with me leniently. The demotion to JSS2 was a just consequence of my actions, and I accepted it with a sense of resignation.

At Aquinas College, every day presented a new opportunity for redemption, a chance to start fresh and earn the trust of my family once again. On their part, my family realized that they had neglected me, leaving me too much to my own devices. They made a conscious effort to mend our relationship. Every six to eight weeks, my father would send me a letter, reminding me of the son of whom I was and a kind of person I was meant to be.

My older brother, Tayo, would often leave his school, Maryhill High School, in Ado Ekiti, and travel to Akure to visit me. He would frequently join me in household chores, providing an opportunity for us to spend quality time together. I was slowly regaining their love and affection. Even my uncle, who had previously shown little interest in my school affairs, began to take an active role in monitoring my progress at school.

My dream was to make my family proud again. While I wasn't the top student at Aquinas College, I made a conscious effort to conduct myself in a manner that would bring honour to my family name. I distanced myself from thuggery and hooliganism, seeking out friends who shared my values. I actively participated in class discussions, asking questions and seeking guidance from my peers. I identified the brightest students among my classmates, such as Familoni Sunday, Sanmi Ajayi, and Muyiwa Awogbami, and formed bonds with them, focusing on our studies together.

Ultimately, we took the Senior Secondary School West African Examinations Council, and I was among the top 25 students out of over

150. I passed all nine subjects, achieving the required five credits, including English and Mathematics needed to proceed for tertiary education. Two years after, in September 1996, I received the news that would forever alter the course of my life: I had been offered a place to study Demography and Social Statistics at the prestigious Obafemi Awolowo University, Ile-Ife. However, due to the relentless industrial action undertaken by university lecturers to demand improved working conditions and infrastructure, my admission was delayed until early 1997.

The university, renowned as the most beautiful in the nation, was a familiar yet exhilarating sight. My father, a porter in one of the halls of residence, had long been a part of this academic community, and my siblings, with the exception of my sister Toyin, had all walked its hallowed grounds. Yet, as a newly minted undergraduate, I felt a unique sense of pride and anticipation. I was no longer a visitor but a student, a member of this prestigious institution, often hailed as "the most beautiful university in the universe."

The year 1996 dawned with the promise of a new chapter. I had finally secured admission to Obafemi Awolowo University, Ile-Ife, a beacon of academic excellence, to embark upon the study of Demography and Social Statistics. However, the relentless industrial actions that gripped the nation's universities, fueled by the faculty's fervent demands for improved working conditions and a revitalization of crumbling infrastructure, cast a long shadow over my eagerly anticipated matriculation. The commencement of academic activities was consequently delayed until the early months of 1997, a period of anxious anticipation that tested the patience of all aspiring undergraduates.

When I finally stepped onto the hallowed grounds of OAU, a sense of awe and wonder washed over me. Though intimately acquainted with the campus, having spent a significant portion of my childhood within its precincts – my father served as a porter in the halls of residence, and my siblings, with the exception of my sister, Toyin, had all pursued their tertiary education within its esteemed walls – this time, the experience was profoundly different. I was no longer a peripheral observer, a fleeting visitor, but a bona fide member of this esteemed institution, often lauded as "the most beautiful university in the universe" by its ardent admirers.

The excitement reached a crescendo as we, the newly minted "Jambitos" – a somewhat pejorative term bestowed upon freshers, a badge of both initiation and insignificance – converged at the foyer of the Faculty of Social Sciences. This was a bittersweet moment, a paradoxical blend of exhilaration and apprehension. We relished the coveted status of being newcomers, yet simultaneously yearned to transcend this ephemeral label, to shed the skin of the neophyte and emerge as seasoned members of the university community. Yet, within this shared experience, a unique camaraderie blossomed, a bond forged in the crucible of shared anticipation and the collective pursuit of academic excellence.

CHAPTER TWO
MY PARENTS

My mother Rachel Omoboja Oluwakiyesi was born in the heart of Ado Ekiti, Nigeria, within the historic Okeyinmi axis. She was born into a family steeped in social prominence and royal lineage. Omoboja's father, Pa Oluwakiyesi, hailed from Ugbaletere, a respected community within the Okeyinmi region. A man of considerable social standing, Pa Oluwakiyesi had carved a niche for himself in the local society. His wife, Omogbolare, a woman of striking beauty and elegance, was a descendant of one of the royal families of Ado Ekiti. Her lineage connected her to the ancient traditions and customs that had shaped the history of the kingdom.

My father is from a great lineage of Oloopetu who left an indelible mark on the community. Benjamin Anuodo, my grandfather and the eldest son of Omole and Aruleola, was a prominent figure in Oke-ila, Ado Ekiti. Renowned for his agricultural prowess, he was also one of the early converts to the Anglican faith in the region. Benjamin's commitment to his faith and his contributions to the community solidified his position as a respected elder.

However, Benjamin's life was not without its challenges. His second wife, Ifariyike, was afflicted by the "Abiku spirit," a malevolent force believed to claim the lives of infants shortly after birth. This belief, prevalent in those days, cast a shadow over the family. History records that my father was born ten times before finally surviving. This extraordinary circumstance, a testament to the resilience of both the child and the family, underscored the profound impact of the Abiku spirit on their lives.

After enduring a series of devastating stillbirths and miscarriages, it was through the unwavering faith and relentless prayers of Fariike and her husband, Anuodo that a glimmer of hope emerged. A revered Aladura, a native prayer warrior, bestowed upon Fariike a sacred bead imbued with spiritual power. Fariike was told to secured this bead around the neck of the next baby, It was believed that it will sever the ties that bound the child to the abiku spirit, the malevolent force that claimed young lives.

Immediately after my father was born, his neck was bound by a spiritual tether, a protective charm meant to ward off the clutches of the abiku spirit who had stolen his life nine times before this attempt. Yet, as he matured, the weight of this supernatural designation grew burdensome. At eight years old, a young and defiant Afolabi cast aside the beads, tossing them into the bush. With this defiant act, he severed the invisible cord that tied him to the spirit world, embracing a life of uncertainty and resilience.

In Yoruba and many African cultures, the tale of the Abiku is woven with threads of myth and reality. A scary practice, often employed by distraught parents, involved marking the body of a deceased child before burial. This grisly ritual was believed to serve as a form of identification, a way to recognize the spirit child should it return to the mortal realm. Once a new child was born into a family haunted by the specter of the Abiku, the parents would anxiously examine the infant's body, searching for any previous markings that might signify its supernatural origin. The discovery of such a mark confirmed the worst fears of the parents, confirming the return of the restless spirit, destined to a cycle of brief life and untimely death.

My father's birth was not formally documented by the local government's vital records office. In the era when he was born, there was only one individual in our neighbourhood who possessed a formal education. This man was entrusted with the task of determining and certifying the birth dates of local children. *abiku*

During my father's childhood, whenever a child sought to enrol in primary school, their parents would approach this man to obtain a verified birth date. He maintained a personal registry wherein he meticulously recorded the birth information of most children in the area. For those whose birth details were not available in his records, he employed historical events or personal anecdotes surrounding their birth to estimate their age and approximate a reasonably accurate birth date.

This man's record showed that my father, Michael Afolabi Anuodo, was born on April 3, 1939. He hailed from the distinguished Oloopetu family of Oke-Ila, Ado Ekiti. His surname, Anuodo, was derived from his father's epithet, "Anuhunlodo-bi-Oyinbo" which translated to "He whoose Orchard is better than a white man's own." This moniker was bestowed upon his father in recognition of his exceptionally well-maintained orchard, which surpassed the quality of those belonging to the British personnel stationed in the area at the time.

During that era, it was common to compare superior attributes to the British, who were often viewed as a symbol of advancement and sophistication. This practice is reflected in names like Omotoyibo, Oguntoyibo, and ifatoyibo, which respectively mean "this child is superior to a British," "the god of iron is greater than a Briton," and "Ifa (a divination system) is more powerful than a Briton." In these contexts, the term "British" was used interchangeably to refer to a white person.

Unlike many Western cultures that place significant emphasis on surnames as a means of identification, the Yoruba culture of south-western Nigeria traditionally prioritizes given names. Surnames were introduced to the Yoruba people as a consequence of colonial influence and the imposition of Western administrative systems. The Yoruba custom is to address individuals by their given names and identify their lineage through their father's name. For example, "Oludare omo Anuodo" translates to "Oludare, son of Anuodo."

On my father's first day of school, he was asked to provide his name. He responded with "Afolabi." Subsequently, he was inquired about his surname or his father's name. My father replied by stating that his father was known as "Anuhunlodo-bi-Oyinbo." The teacher found this name unusual and cumbersome, as it was considerably longer than the surnames they were accustomed to. In a display of ingenuity, the teacher devised a shortened version of the name, resulting in the surname "Anuodo" that my father and subsequent generations have carried.

My father's mother, Elizabeth Fariyike, hailed from the esteemed Elemukanse chieftaincy family, a prominent district within the city of Ado Ekiti. The Elemukanse title held immense power and prestige within the Ado Ekiti community. The individual bearing this title was a revered figure, renowned for his exceptional bravery and military prowess. He had participated in numerous battles, valiantly defending the township and securing victories that contributed to its strength and prosperity.

Afolabi, the first son of his parents, was baptized at the historic St. Andrew's Church Okeyinmi, Ado Ekiti where he received the

Christian name Michael. This act of faith marked the beginning of a new chapter in the family's journey, a chapter filled with hope and the promise of a brighter future.

MY PARENTS' LOVE STORY

The love story of Afolabi and Omoboja was a tale of serendipitous encounter and enduring affection. Their paths crossed in the hallowed halls of St. Andrew's Church, Okeyinmi in 1961. At the tender ages of 18 and 22, Omoboja found herself captivated by the charm and charisma of the tall and handsome-looking Afolabi, who would later become her husband. Their connection was immediate, and their love blossomed amidst the serene ambiance of the church.

Two years after their initial meeting, in 1963, Afolabi and Omoboja exchanged vows in the same church where their love story had begun. Their union was a celebration of youth, love, and hope. As they embarked on their journey together, they were both filled with anticipation for the future.

In the same year of their marriage, Afolabi and Omogbolare welcomed their first child, a son they named Gbenga. The arrival of Gbenga brought immense joy and fulfillment to the young couple. Their family was growing, and their love for each other deepened with each passing day. My parents' love story was a tale woven with threads of love, sacrifice, and unwavering dedication. Their marriage, though unconventional by modern standards, was a testament to the enduring power of love and shared values.

In an era when public displays of affection were frowned upon, their love blossomed quietly, nurtured by mutual respect and understanding. As a child, I witnessed little in the way of romantic gestures or tender expressions of love between them. Yet, their bond was undeniable, a silent symphony of love that resonated through our family. Despite the absence of outward displays of affection, my parents were undeniably devoted to each other.

Their marriage, blessed with seven children, was a testament to their shared faith and unwavering commitment to their family. Both deeply religious individuals, they were pillars of their community, setting an example of integrity and compassion. One of the defining characteristics of my parents' relationship was the geographical distance that often separated them. While my father worked in Ile-Ife, a university town in present-day Osun State, my mother remained in our hometown of Ado Ekiti, the capital of Ekiti State. Despite the physical distance, their love remained steadfast, and my father made frequent trips home to be with his beloved wife.

Education was a paramount concern for my parents. They harboured a deep-seated belief in the transformative power of education and were determined to provide their children with the opportunities they themselves had been denied. My father, in particular, made a solemn vow to God that all of his children would attain university degrees and become respected citizens like his cousins, the Osiberus of Shagamu, Ogun State. I recall a poignant incident that underscored my parents' unwavering commitment to our education. Our cherished black and white television, a prized possession in our humble home, mysteriously disappeared from its stand in 1985. While my father initially attributed the disappearance to a technical malfunction, we later discovered the truth; he had used it as collateral to secure a loan to support his eldest son, who was pursuing his studies at the University of Ife.

My mother, too, made extraordinary sacrifices to support our education. She sold everything she could to ensure we had the resources we needed to succeed. No matter what we asked for, as long as it was related to our studies, she would do her utmost to provide it. My parents' unwavering dedication to education was inspired by the example of my mother's cousins, the Olas. These educated individuals, who held prestigious white-collar jobs, served as role models for us. My mother often encouraged us to emulate them, urging us to strive for excellence and make our mark on the world. Despite the hardships we faced, my parents' love and resilience remained unwavering. They faced adversity with courage and determination, their Christian faith serving as a beacon of hope in the darkest of times.

MY MOTHER'S DEATH: THE SPECTRE OF STROKE

In the early 1990s, a devastating event struck our family. While attending a family wedding, my mother suffered a stroke. The sudden onset of this debilitating condition left her unable to talk, walk or use her right hand and leg. The news of her illness sent shockwaves through our family and the community. My father, who had always relied heavily on my mother's support, was devastated by her illness. The children, too, were heartbroken, questioning why God would afflict such a devoted and selfless woman. The loss of my mother's catering business, a significant source of income for our family, compounded our challenges.

The spectre of stroke cast a long shadow over our family for three arduous years 1990-1993. Omoboja, a woman of indomitable spirit, struggled valiantly against the debilitating effects of hypertension. It was a harrowing ordeal, particularly for her, who found it difficult to reconcile her sickness with her unwavering faith in God. She clung to her prayers with unwavering devotion, reciting the familiar lines, "Olorun da eje re bo mi, Jesu Feje re wemi," seeking solace in the belief that she was protected by the blood of Jesus. Her unwavering faith was a beacon of hope for us all, even in the darkest of times.

On the 8th of July, 1993, an unsettling event transpired. My mother, seemingly possessed by an inexplicable force, began urging everyone to pack their belongings. She spoke of a celestial bus waiting to transport the faithful to her heavenly Father's kingdom. Hours passed as she repeated this peculiar message, her voice growing increasingly faint. As her words trailed off, she began to confess a particular phrase, "Oluwa so mi dasegun," meaning "God has made me a victorious child." It was a chilling display, leaving us all deeply concerned.

At about 5 PM, a sense of tranquillity descended upon her. She began to pray for each of her children, starting with Gbenga, her eldest, and ending with Tosin, her youngest. After offering prayers for her beloved husband, she took her last breath and slipped away, leaving us in a state of profound grief. Wails echoed through our home as we mourned the loss of our beloved mother. Why had such a terrible fate befallen her? Why must the good suffer while the wicked thrive? Our hearts were heavy with sorrow, and our minds raced with unanswered questions.

The loss of our mother was a devastating blow to our family. She was the cornerstone of our lives, the woman who held us together. Her absence left a void that could never be filled. As we mourned her passing, we found solace in the memories of her love and resilience. She had fought bravely against adversity, her faith serving as a beacon of hope in the darkest of times.

We surely missed her dearly, but we knew that she was at peace, reunited with her heavenly Father. We would carry her memory with us always, honouring her legacy of love, strength, and unwavering faith. As the sun set on that fateful day, the news of her death travelled around. It was a day never to be forgotten. Till date, her passing was a profound loss, but it also served as a reminder of the fragility of life and the importance of cherishing every moment. May her soul continues to rest in eternal peace.

MY FATHER'S LEGACY, SECOND MARRIAGE AND BATTLE WITH CANCER

In the wake of my mother's untimely passing in 1993, my father made a solemn vow. He pledged to remain single, dedicating himself entirely to raising us, his children. This was a promise born of love and a shared dream with my mother to ensure our educational success, to guide us through the labyrinth of academia.

Year after year, he steadfastly honored his commitment. No woman graced his life, a solitary figure navigating the complexities of single parenthood. As I pen these words, long after his own departure, questions linger unanswered. Did he truly remain alone, or did a secret companion provide solace and support? Perhaps, in the quiet moments of reflection, I may have sought answers to these mysteries, but alas, he is no longer here to share his story.

In the year 2001, as our youngest sibling, Tosin, prepared to embark on his university journey to study Law, we recognized the need for companionship in our father's life. With Tosin soon to leave the house, we knew that our father would face the challenge of living alone, a solitary figure in a house once filled with life. We encouraged him to consider finding a partner, someone who could provide comfort and support.

Our father, a man of faith, sought guidance from his church. There, he met a woman who, like him, had experienced the complexities of marriage and divorce. Despite their shared pasts, they found solace and love in each other. With the blessing of the church and the support of our family, including my late uncle, Pastor Opeyemi Anuodo, they were united in holy matrimony.

The years that followed were filled with happiness and contentment. Our father and his new wife settled in Ile-Ife, enjoying a peaceful and fulfilling life together. However, in 2010, a significant change occurred. My elder brother, Tayo, built a beautiful house in our hometown of Ado Ekiti, a tangible expression of his love and devotion. With great joy, our father and his wife relocated to their new home, a testament to the transformative power of family.

My father, a beacon of wisdom and generosity, commanded the respect of his peers at Ado Ekiti. The children he nurtured to become university graduates became his legacy, a testament to his enduring influence. He was a man of abundance, not just in material possessions, but in the lives he touched. A source of blessing to countless individuals, his generosity knew no bounds, as he received money from his children, he spread the love in his community.

In 2014, after he celebrated his 75th birthday in an elaborate style, fate dealt him a cruel blow. He was diagnosed with prostate enlargement, a condition that, due to mismanaged treatment, led to an unusual complication: the enlargement of his breasts. This unexpected development culminated in a rare form of breast cancer. Despite the adversity, he faced his illness with courage and grace, receiving the necessary care and support, enduring countless hospital stays with unwavering fortitude.

As he marked his 80th birthday in 2019, a quiet contemplation settled upon him. He confided in me, his voice tinged with a sense of peace that he was ready to embark on his final journey. He longed to reunite with his beloved wife, Omoboja, and their cherished son, Gbenga. Though my heart ached at the thought of losing him, I clung to hope, insisting that he would celebrate many more birthdays, his wisdom a guiding light for generations to come.

The year 2020, a year etched in infamy, was marked by the relentless grip of the COVID-19 pandemic. As the world grappled with this unseen enemy, claiming millions of lives, our family faced a different kind of crisis. In the summer of that year, my father's health took a perilous turn.

On the 15th of July, 2020, I received a call from sister Toyin that my father's health had began to deteriorate. Sister Yemisi and I, both residents of Ile-Ife, were compelled to seek special permission to travel to Ado Ekiti, defying the stringent interstate travel restrictions imposed by the government. Upon our arrival in Ado Ekiti, a wave of relief washed over my father's face. His fear of dying without seeing us, a haunting specter, had been allayed.

My sister, Toyin, who had relocated from the turbulent North due to the Boko Haram insurgency, was a constant source of comfort and care. She tirelessly attended to his needs, driving him to countless medical appointments. Her unwavering dedication was a beacon of hope in those trying times.

As I beheld my father, a shadow of his former self, a pang of sorrow pierced my heart. The insidious cancer had ravaged his once robust frame, reducing him to a mere shell. Yet, his spirit remained unbroken. In a voice weakened by illness, he expressed his readiness to depart, to reunite with his beloved wife, Omoboja, and their firstborn son, Gbenga. Though my heart ached at the thought of losing him, I could only offer words of comfort and love, hoping to prolong his earthly existence.

Sister Yemisi, ever mindful of spiritual matters, inquired if my father harbored any resentment towards anyone, urging him to release any lingering bitterness to ensure a clear path to the afterlife. He confessed to harboring feelings of resentment towards a cousin, a respected figure in a prominent Nigerian church. Prompted by my sister, he extended forgiveness, a gesture he solidified by placing a phone call to his cousin and offering a heartfelt prayer.

Even in his weakened state of physical health, his mind remained sharp. He took turns praying for each of us, his blessings encompassing even the youngest of his grandchildren. He mentioned by names all the daughters and son in-law and prayed for them. Yet, a pang of sadness clouded his eyes as he spoke of Tayo, his beloved son who had relocated to Canada. The COVID-19 pandemic had cruelly prevented a long-awaited reunion, due to ban on international travels, this remained a source of deep regret for him. We contacted through phone, Tayo, who had been in regular communication with my father. Despite their daily conversations, he was overjoyed to speak with him directly, with all of us gathered around. It was a heartwarming moment, a testament to the enduring bond between father and son, even across the miles.

In his wisdom, he expressed his final wishes, requesting that his mortal remains not be kept in the mortuary for more than two weeks. He also indicated the precise spot where he wished to be laid to rest, a final act of earthly planning.

We left for Ile-Ife that same evening, our hearts heavy with the weight of impending loss. A week later, on the somber morning, around 0200 hours of July 22nd, 2020, a chilling phone call from Sister Toyin shattered our world. Our beloved father had departed, his spirit soaring to the heavens.

In his final hours, a profound sense of peace washed over him. His youngest sister had visited and opted to sleep over, and in a moment of profound clarity, my dad had requested to be moved from the comfort of his bed to the bare floor, a simple, earthy return to the elements. His family, initially hesitant, sought counsel from my father's sister, Auntie Bose. She, a woman of deep spiritual insight, recognized the signs. She spoke of a life intertwined with the spirit world. As a child, my father, an abiku, had defied the forces that sought to claim him, casting into the bush, the protective beads meant to tether him. Guided by her wisdom, the family made a difficult decision.

They laid him gently upon a duvet on the floor, a final act of love and respect. As he drifted into a peaceful sleep, a sense of tranquility filled the room. Yet, as the night deepened, his breath faltered, and the silence that followed was a stark reminder of the fragility of life. In the quiet hours of the morning around 1am, his breath stilled, and a mournful silence fell.

The Yoruba adage, "Emo ku, oju opo di, eye lo, ori ite dofo," echoed through our hearts. A grasscutter dies, leaving an empty burrow. A bird perishes, its nest forsaken. So too, our father had departed, leaving an irreplaceable void in our lives. The end of an era.

A fortnight after his passing, a solemn yet fitting funeral service was held to honor his memory. Despite the ongoing threat of the Covid-19 pandemic, a multitude gathered to pay their final respects to this illustrious son of Ado Ekiti. Among the mourners was Professor Ishola Olomola, a lifelong friend who had walked beside him through every chapter of his life. Many traveled from Ile-Ife, including Professor Oluwatosin, his former pastor, to bid their farewell.

As we mourn his loss, we find solace in the hymns that once filled his life. A particular favorite, Hymn 15869 from The Cyber Hymnal, echoes through our hearts:

1 A o pa de leti odo,
T'ese angeli ti te;
T'o mo gara bi kristali;

Leba ite olorun?

Egbe:

A o pade leti odo

Odo didan, odo didan na

Pel' awon mimo leba odo

T'o nsan leba ite ni.

2 Leti bebe odo na yi

Pel' Olusaguntan wa,

A o ma rin a o ma sin

B'a ti ntele 'pase Re. [Egbe]

3 K'a to de odo didan naa,

A o s'eru wa kale

Jesu y'o gba eru ese

Awon ti y'o de l'ade. [Egbe]

4 Nje l'eba odo tutu na,

A o r'oju Olugbala;

Emi wa ki o pinya mo

Yi o korin ogo Re. [Egbe]

CHAPTER THREE
MY UNDERGRADUATE
EXPERIENCE

My undergraduate days at Obafemi Awolowo University was a blend of vibrant crucible of intellectual and social life, notable with remarkable events, and enduring memories. Indeed, to encapsulate the fullness of that era within the confines of a single tome would be a Herculean task, yet I shall endeavor to capture its essence, to distill the unforgettable happenings that indelibly marked my time there.

From the very inception of our academic pursuits, my class, a throng of over 150 eager minds, discerned in me a nascent leadership potential. With a remarkable unanimity, they bestowed upon me the mantle of Class Representative, appointing me as the vital liaison between our esteemed lecturers and my fellow classmates.

This role, though seemingly modest, rapidly catapulted me into the limelight among the Jambite of my set. In each lecture theatre, I became a veritable conduit of information, disseminating crucial updates and insights to my classmates. This popularity inevitably drew me into the tempestuous waters of student union politics. Despite my fervent engagement in these extra-curricular pursuits, I maintained an unwavering commitment to my academic endeavors. At the culmination of the first year, I emerged triumphant in all my courses, a testament to my dedication and diligence.

At the conclusion of my second year, I boldly entered the fray, contesting for the esteemed position of Director of Socials at Obafemi Awolowo Hall, the political headquarters of campus politics, the hallowed ground where the political pulse of the university truly beat, the epicenter of student welfare and the crucible of resistance against perceived oppression perpetrated by the university management. The electoral battle was fierce, a clash of wills and ideologies, but ultimately, I emerged victorious, securing a landslide victory.

My undergraduate odyssey was not solely confined to the hallowed halls of academia and the turbulent seas of student politics. It was also a period of romantic exploration, a time for experimentation and the cultivation of meaningful lessons for life relationship. I embarked upon a series of campus romances, each a unique chapter in the intricate narrative of my personal growth. To preserve the sanctity of these intimate experiences, I shall refrain from divulging the identities of those involved.

CAMPUS ROMANCE

My freshman year was a whirlwind of youthful exuberance. I found myself drawn to three captivating individuals, each possessing a unique allure. The first, whom I shall refer to as "Seventeen," was a student of the Department of Political Science. Our paths first crossed during the first year registration exercise, and a peculiar magnetism soon blossomed between us.

Her petite frame and unwavering confidence captivated my attention. She exuded an air of youthful independence, a free spirit seemingly unburdened by the weight of the world. My initial interactions were marked by an awkwardness that bordered on the impetuous, culminating in a rather inauspicious query: "Are you here to visit your elder sibling, or have you come to join us?" Her response, delivered with a surprising maturity that belied her childlike appearance, was swift and to the point: "You are quite rude, sir. I am a freshman, just like you."

Despite her sharp rebuke, her voice, strong and confident, held an undeniable charm. I confessed my burgeoning affection, but she gently declined, citing her parents' wishes for academic focus, deferring romantic pursuits until her final year. While I yearned for immediate reciprocation, I respected her decision and cherished the blossoming friendship that ensued. We shared moments of simple joy, savouring popcorn during late-night movie screenings and forging a bond built on mutual respect and understanding.

Another captivating figure entered my life about the same time that I was seeing Seventeen: a radiant young woman from the Department of Economics whom I shall call "Yetty." Our paths crossed unexpectedly one evening as I returned to my dormitory. A sense of instant attraction, a fleeting spark of infatuation, ignited between us. We gravitated towards each other, our interactions filled with unspoken desires and hesitant glances. Yet, youthful timidity held us captive. I yearned to articulate my feelings, to express the depth of my affection, but the fear of rejection, of jeopardising the fragile bond we had already formed, kept me paralysed.

Our time together was filled with intimate moments, shared confidences, and a silent understanding that transcended the spoken word. While we never formally embarked on a romantic pursuit, a profound connection blossomed between us, a testament to the unspoken language of the heart.

Lastly, by the second semester of my first year, fate again brought me into the orbit of another remarkable lady, a law student whom I shall refer to as "Delaw." The daughter of a prominent figure in my home state, her father was a University Professor and a renowned politician. Delaw exuded an aura of sophistication and grace. Our friendship flourished rapidly, marked by frequent visits to each other's rooms, engaging conversations, and the camaraderie forged with her roommates and classmates.

While many of my peers struggled to navigate the complexities of campus romance, I found myself surrounded by a constellation of captivating women, each unique and intriguing in their own way. My role as Class Representative, coupled with my active engagement in student life, further enhanced my social standing, drawing a circle of female friends around me. I had become, in the eyes of my peers, a veritable "star boy," a figure of admiration and envy.

My third year at Obafemi Awolowo University unfolded with a vibrant tapestry of academic pursuits and unexpected romantic entanglements. Two captivating women, Lola and Lade, entered the stage of my heart. Lola, a student in the Faculty of Administration, possessed a striking beauty and an intellect that ignited my curiosity. Lade, a vibrant soul from the Faculty of Education, captured my attention with her infectious energy and radiant smile.

My encounter with Lade occurred during a captivating campus Christian concert organised by the Cherubs and Seraphim Fellowship. The legendary Ayo ni O choir, whose soul-stirring melodies had enchanted my childhood, graced the stage that fateful evening. One of their timeless anthems, "*Emi ti wo kari aye yii boya emi yio rii, enikan to ga ju o lo*" (a poignant reflection on the ultimate supremacy of God), resonated deeply within me, evoking a profound sense of nostalgia.

The concert was a vibrant spectacle of music, dance, and exuberant joy. As the choir performed a medley of old school favourites, the atmosphere crackled with excitement. Students swayed and danced, their spirits lifted by the infectious rhythm. Amidst this sea of revelers, I noticed a petite figure, a vision of grace and energy, dancing with an infectious enthusiasm. In the endearing vernacular of my Yoruba heritage, she could be aptly described as "*a kuru yejo, obirin ruburubu,*" a petite and vivacious woman. Despite the perspiration that beaded on her brow, her smile remained radiant, illuminating the space around her.

Driven by an irresistible impulse, I navigated the throng of students and found myself dancing beside her. Her warmth and grace were palpable, and despite the stark contrast in our heights, a comfortable camaraderie quickly blossomed. "My name is Dare, a 300 level, Demography and Statistics student" I introduced myself, my voice a mixture of excitement and apprehension. "I'm Lade," she replied, her voice melodious and her smile reassuring. "I'm in my third year, studying English Education." She informed me that she was a dedicated member of the fellowship that had organised the concert. I, on the other hand, had stumbled upon the event quite serendipitously, drawn by the alluring poster that adorned the campus notice board.

As the concert drew to a close, we parted ways, each of us returning to our respective hostels. Although the image of Lade, her vibrant spirit and captivating smile, lingered in my mind, other pursuits soon occupied my attention. I had already become entangled in a romantic pursuit with Lola, a diploma student in the Department of Local Government Studies. Introduced to me by my roommates, Lola possessed a captivating beauty, her striking features accentuated by her robust curvaceous figure. Hailing from Ado Ekiti, my hometown, she also boasted a privileged background, her father a renowned Islamic cleric.

The echoes of the concert lingered, their vibrant melodies haunting my every waking moment. Lade, the enigmatic figure who had captivated my heart that night, became an inescapable presence in my thoughts. Days bled into weeks, each one a torment of yearning. My confidante, Yomi Amoloja, a fellow student of Economics in his third year, had been my companion at the concert. He, too, had been smitten, though his affections had found a different target – Lade's vivacious friend.

He recounted their burgeoning romance with a mischievous glint in his eye, confessing that Lade frequently inquired about me during their outings. Intrigued by this revelation, I decided to make a move.

One evening, I accompanied Yomi to Mozambique Hall, the abode of these captivating young women. I prepared meticulously for this encounter, adorning myself in my finest attire, the scent of a modest, albeit counterfeit, perfume mingling with the faint trace of powder I had applied to my face, a desperate attempt to appear fresh and alluring. As we entered the room, my gaze immediately fell upon Lade. She approached me with a radiant smile, enveloping me in a warm embrace.

Our conversation flowed easily, punctuated by shared laughter and insightful observations. Finally, I seized the opportunity, confessing my burgeoning affection for her. To my delight, she reciprocated, albeit with a caveat: a strictly platonic relationship, devoid of any romantic intimacy. Eager to bask in her presence, I readily agreed. Thus began our unconventional courtship. We became inseparable companions, attending concerts together, sharing cinematic experiences, and indulging in delectable meals at the university's finest eateries.

However, navigating this delicate arrangement required meticulous planning. Both Lade and Lola resided within the confines of Mozambique Hall, and I became a master of discreet timing, ensuring their paths never crossed, a silent guardian of this carefully constructed charade.

The clandestine nature of my rendezvous with Lade began to cast a long shadow over my burgeoning friendship with Lola. A subtle shift had crept into her demeanour, a newfound intensity in her gaze, a lingering silence that spoke volumes. She sensed a discordant note, a dissonance in the harmony of our companionship, though the precise source of her unease remained elusive. Determined to unravel the mystery, she began to weave herself more tightly into the fabric of my daily life, her presence a constant, particularly in the evenings, the very hours I had tacitly reserved for my clandestine meetings with Lade.

The truth, a bitter pill to swallow, was that my heart, though drawn to the allure of Lola's beauty – her statuesque frame, her voluptuous curves, her undeniable affluence – remained irrevocably tethered to Lade. Lola, with her inherent generosity, sought to nourish my well-being, both physically and emotionally. "My mother will be sending our family driver with a generous supply of meat," she announced one evening, her voice tinged with a warmth that both charmed and troubled me. "I shall prepare a delectable soup with it and deliver it to you, ensuring you are well-nourished." I feigned enthusiasm, assuring her that I eagerly anticipated the culinary delight.

That very evening, however, Lade had extended an invitation to a spiritual gathering, a "Night of Effective Prayer and Deliverance" at her church. My heart, ever drawn to her, readily accepted. "Perhaps I can collect you on my way," she suggested, her voice laced with a hint of anticipation. I, consumed by a burgeoning sense of guilt, resorted to a convenient lie, claiming I would be making my way directly from the academic enclave to the designated venue – the university's expansive sports arena.

By 9 p.m., the hour of my rendezvous with Lade drawing near, I felt the weight of Lola's concern pressing down upon me. With a mixture of guilt and impatience, I extricated myself from her company, feigning a pressing academic obligation – a forthcoming examination that demanded immediate attention. Though she voiced her reluctance, her gentle nature ultimately yielded, allowing me to escape the confines of her watchful gaze.

The air in the prayer hall was thick with the fervour of fervent supplication. A blend of voices, some raised in impassioned pleas, others murmuring in hushed reverence, filled the space. I, a latecomer to this spiritual gathering, quietly slipped into the congregation, my own approach to prayer a stark contrast to the exuberant displays around me. I have never been one for histrionics, for bombastic pronouncements before the divine. In my humble opinion, prayer should be a conversation, an intimate dialogue with the Creator, much like the supplications one offers to an earthly father – a respectful plea, not a demanding shout.

With this philosophy in mind, I began to pour out my heart to the Almighty, entrusting my academic pursuits and my future to His benevolent guidance. I implored Him to grant me the unwavering focus necessary to excel in my studies, and most crucially, I beseeched Him for the courage to extricate myself from the emotional entanglement with Lola, a necessary step towards cultivating a deeper connection with Lade.

Suddenly, the noise subsided, replaced by an eerie silence. Then, a voice, otherworldly in its cadence, pierced the stillness. It was a woman, speaking in an unknown tongue, her voice weaving through the crowd, pausing momentarily at each individual, as if delivering a personal message from the divine. Beside her, an interpreter translated the cryptic utterances, while another diligently recorded the prophetic pronouncements.

Standing somewhat apart from the throng, I observed this spectacle with a degree of skepticism. The theatrics of these spiritual gathering, with their emphasis on divine pronouncements and supernatural interventions, often left me unconvinced. The notion of a divine messenger, an "*Elemi*" as they were often called, conveying cryptic messages from the celestial realm, struck me as somewhat far-fetched. Yet, as the woman approached me, her gaze piercing through the crowd, a shiver of apprehension ran down my spine.

"Li kaka kum ka... Maleika yakhum...(unknown tongue)" she intoned, her voice a low, resonant hum. The words, though

incomprehensible, carried an undeniable weight, a sense of impending doom. The interpreter, his voice grave, delivered the chilling message: "A warning from above. A soup of destruction, *'obe iparun,'* is coming your way." Terror gripped me. My mind raced back to a conversation with Lola earlier that day. She had excitedly mentioned her intention to prepare a special soup for me, using the fried meat her mother would be sending from home.

The coincidence, if it could be called that, was unsettling. A spiritualist, a purveyor of the divine, warning me against consuming unknown soups, and mere moments prior, Lola, the very embodiment of my romantic entanglements, had offered me a culinary offering. The scripture, a beacon of solace, had always promised "fullness of joy in the house of God." Yet, that evening, I emerged from the service a vessel adrift in a sea of confusion and despair. The chilling phrase *"Obe Iparun"* – "Soup of Destruction" echoed through my mind, a venomous serpent gnawing at my peace. "Why me?" The question, a mournful lament, reverberated through my soul, unanswered.

How could Lola, the girl I believed loved me, harbour such malevolent intentions? To conspire against me, to unleash diabolical forces through this sinister *"Obe Iparun"* – the very thought was a revelation of unimaginable cruelty. After the programme, Lade, her face etched with concern, approached me. "Which of your girlfriends is bringing you soup?" she teased, her playful banter a stark contrast to the distressing prophecy I had just endured. Sensing my distress, her tone shifted. "Be careful," she urged, her eyes filled with a newfound gravity. "I don't want to lose you." I sought her opinion on the Elemi's unsettling revelation. "Of course I believe it," she declared with unwavering conviction.

The weight of the Elemi's words, coupled with Lade's sobering confirmation, cast a long shadow over the remainder of the evening. As I tossed and turned on my narrow mattress, sleep remained an elusive refuge. The specter of "*Obe Iparun*" loomed large, a chilling reminder of the insidious forces that lurked beneath the surface of human relationships.

"Sleep eluded me that night, my mind a tempest of anxieties that tossed me from side to side. Finally, exhaustion yielded a meager respite, perhaps three hours of fitful sleep before the dawn. As the first rays of light pierced the gloom, a single thought crystallised:

I must seek my father's counsel. Though typically self-reliant, I felt a profound need for his guidance. This was no trivial matter; its gravity weighed heavily upon my soul. I clung to the hope that his wisdom, honed by a lifetime of experience, would illuminate a path through the darkness.

A poignant Yoruba proverb echoed in my mind: *Tomode ba peku, a daaje. Tomode ba peja, a daaje, ojo tomode ba aro gidigba, a gbe wale fun baba re*" meaning when a child hunts a grass-cutter, he feasts alone, when he captures fish, he enjoys the spoils himself, but when a child kills the elusive *aro gidigba*, a creature of the deep sea, offspring of the formidable Yemoja, the powerful deity of the ocean, he must present his catch to his father."

The *aro gidigba,* a mythical creature of immense power and beauty, symbolizes a challenge beyond the ordinary. Just as the child, humbled by the extraordinary nature of his catch, seeks his father's wisdom, so too did I, facing an unprecedented dilemma, turn to the wellspring of my father's experience, seeking solace and guidance in his unwavering support.

The weight of my father's disappointment settled upon me like a shroud. My youthful indiscretion, a reckless emotional entanglement with not one, but two ladies, instead of focusing on my studies, a grievous offense in his eyes. His words, though laced with a gruff affection, were a sharp rebuke. "You have brought this mess upon yourself, my son," he declared, his voice a low rumble. "Had this prophecy remained a distant murmur, I might have counseled you to disregard it. But you, with your own ears, heard its gloomy prophecy. Now, heed the warning." His advice, a bitter pill, was tempered by a love that sought to steer me away from the precipice of self-destruction. Days later, Lola, the enigmatic lady at the heart of this predicament, arrived bearing a mysterious offering, a modest aluminum pot brimming with a rich, beefy stew. With the stealth of a serpent, she had slipped it into my cupboard, leaving a cryptic note on my bed.

Returning to my room late that evening, weary and famished, I found myself facing a stark dilemma. My stomach rumbled, a primal urge demanding sustenance. I had even purchased a loaf of bread, a meager consolation, intending to make do with a simple meal of bread dipped in water. But then, I saw it – the pot of stew, a tantalizing beacon of warmth and comfort, yet a potential harbinger of doom.

The chilling words of my father, the whispers of superstition, echoed in my mind, a chilling counterpoint to the seductive aroma. I wrestled with temptation, the savory scent a cruel torment, but ultimately, caution prevailed. I ate my bread, the taste of simple sustenance a stark reminder of the consequences of my own folly.

The following morning, I recounted the events to my roommates, the boisterous Banji Bosun (late), whose laughter echoed through our shared space, the ever-present Kunle Internet, the elder Baba Victor, a man of quiet wisdom, and my younger brother, Femi, a frequent visitor to my room. Banji, ever the daredevil, declared his intention to partake of the forbidden stew. "It's meant to destroy you, not me," he proclaimed with a mischievous glint in his eye, his bravado masking a hint of trepidation.

Bosun and my other roommates ravenously devoured the soup, consuming every morsel of meat within. Though the aroma was undeniably enticing, I steadfastly resisted the urge to partake. I had been solemnly warned, and I would not jeopardize my life for a mere bowl of soup.

My relationship with Lola irrevocably fractured. I began to deliberately distance myself, feigning absence whenever she visited. I would flee her presence or seek refuge within, instructing my roommates to convey my unavailability. She sensed my deliberate avoidance, yet was powerless to alter my course.

One evening, two of her closest confidantes arrived, imploring me to visit her. They claimed she was gravely ill, both emotionally and physically, and believed my presence was the sole remedy. Reluctantly, I consented. Upon my arrival, she was overcome by a torrent of tears, lamenting her perceived transgressions. "What have I done wrong?" she sobbed, "Why have you forsaken me?" I lacked a definitive answer, unable to divulge the unsettling revelations of the *'obe iparun'*. Consoled by my presence, I offered a pragmatic explanation to end our relationship, citing the imperative of academic focus and the need to eliminate all distractions. Though the parting was bittersweet, I felt a sense of closure, having formally severed our connection."

The ensuing weeks saw a deliberate distancing from Lola, a severing of the ties that bound us.

Concurrently, my connection with Lade deepened. I introduced her to my family, a momentous step. My siblings, and even my father, met her with a guarded warmth. Though their acceptance was evident, an undercurrent of doubt persisted. They sensed an inherent incompatibility, a misalignment of our stars. I acknowledged their concerns, but the yearning for a stable, uncomplicated relationship, especially after the tumultuous affair with Lola, had me grasping at this fragile connection. The weight of my final year loomed, and the need to focus on my studies, to navigate the turbulent waters of academia, became paramount."

JULY10 1999: OAU MASSACRE

Obafemi Awolowo University's preeminence among Nigerian institutions rests not solely on the grandeur of its architectural marvels, nor exclusively on its esteemed academic pedigree. A defining factor lies in its relative immunity from the scourge of campus cultism. During the 1990s, when tales of cult-related violence permeated the nation's higher education landscape, OAU remained a beacon of tranquility. Students traversed the campus at all hours, unhindered by the specter of fear, freely pursuing their intellectual endeavors within the hallowed halls of academia.

At Obafemi Awolowo University, the vibrant hum of intellectual pursuit extended far beyond the confines of the classroom. Each night, the lecture theaters is transformed into bustling reading rooms. Students, drawn from the farthest reaches of the campus, from the distant Mozambique and Angola Hostels, converged upon these sanctuaries of knowledge. They would pore over textbooks, their faces illuminated by the soft glow of ceiling lights, some persevering until the early hours of the morning, the clock striking two or three before they reluctantly retreated to their hostels, seeking a few precious hours of sleep before the dawn of another academic day.

While the specter of secret societies loomed large, their activities remained shrouded in an air of mystique. The presence of fraternities like the Black Axe, the Eye, the Pirates, and the Buccaneers was undeniable, whispers of their existence circulating amongst the student body. Yet, these groups operated with a calculated discretion, their rituals and meetings conducted in the shadows, a deliberate avoidance of any overt display that might expose them to the scrutiny of the university authorities or the watchful eyes of the student union.

Despite their secrecy, however, the student union, ever vigilant, occasionally intercepted intelligence regarding their gatherings, swiftly moving to disrupt their clandestine activities. Obafemi Awolowo Hall, a crucible of student activism, served as the nerve center of campus politics. Its hallowed grounds housed successive generations of student union leaders, their spirits imbued with the fiery spirit of dissent. The hall's denizens, a breed apart, were renowned for their political fervor, their voices the first to rise in any clamor against perceived injustices. Whenever discord erupted between the university administration and the student body, the flames of protest, the dreaded 'Aluta,' invariably ignited within Awolowo Hall's walls. As a member of the hall's executive council, I was drawn into the vortex of campus politics, my position as Director of Social thrusting me into the limelight. My role, to orchestrate the social fabric of 'Awo boys,' as we were affectionately known, endeared me to my peers.

An incident in March 1999 etched itself indelibly into our collective memory. Awo boys, in a daring operation, apprehended a clandestine cult within the confines of the Senior Staff Quarters. The den, a chilling testament to the dangers lurking beneath the veneer of academia, yielded a cache of automatic rifles and shotguns, a chilling reminder of the forces at play. The apprehended cultists were brought to Awo Hall, not as prisoners, but as subjects of a swift and unconventional justice system.

For years, the university administration had failed to inspire confidence in its ability to uphold the law. Student trust had eroded, replaced by a cynical distrust. This vacuum, however, had been filled by a burgeoning sense of self-governance. Awo Hall Coffee Room, in a sense, had become the custodian of justice, a microcosm of a society grappling with the limitations of established authority."

The student justice system, a time-honored tradition passed down through generations, recognized three distinct levels of punishment. *'Feerefe shishi'* – a swift, corrective beating with a cane or belt – was reserved for minor transgressions, a swift reprimand before the student was released. *'Minimum shishi'* – a more severe punishment involving one or two slaps – followed by immediate release, served as a deterrent for more serious offenses. Finally, *'maximum shishi,'* the ultimate sanction, was reserved for the most egregious crimes, such as involvement in cult activities.

Intelligence reports surfaced to the Students Union, painting a grim picture: a cabal of cultists planned to unleash chaos upon the campus. This intelligence galvanized the Awo boys into action. A swift and decisive response was necessary to thwart the impending mayhem. A clandestine operation ensued, culminating in the apprehension of about ten suspected cultists. Armed with sophisticated weaponry, they posed a grave threat to the campus community. Brought before the student tribunal, in the dreaded Awo Hall Coffee Room, they faced the full weight of *'maximum shishi.'* The punishment was swift and brutal, a harrowing ordeal of severe physical torment. Following this, the cultists were handed over to the university security, their fate sealed as they awaited further processing by the state police.

The interrogation of the arrested cultists, conducted by a cadre of determined students, Led by the Secretary General Of the Student Union; Commrade 'Yemi Iwilade George aka Afrika yielded a bombshell: a high-ranking figure within the university administration, a pillar of the institution itself, was implicated as the patron of a notorious cult group operating within the campus. This revelation ignited a firestorm. Students, their sense of justice and trust irrevocably shattered, embarked on a peaceful protest, their voices rising in a chorus of dissent.

The university administration, however, met this display of student power with an iron fist.

In a swift and decisive move, the campus was abruptly shuttered, its vibrant life abruptly silenced for two weeks. The reopening of the university was a somber affair. The air crackled with tension, the echoes of the recent upheaval still reverberating. The administration, seeking to quell any further dissent, issued a draconian set of regulations. The student union, a bastion of student voice and advocacy, was unceremoniously suspended, its power effectively neutered.

Furthermore, a chilling edict was issued: gatherings of more than four students were strictly prohibited across the entire campus, with the sole exception of sanctioned lectures. This draconian measure, intended to stifle dissent, cast a long shadow over the campus, an oppressive reminder of the administration's newfound authoritarianism.

The university, once a sanctuary of free thought and intellectual discourse, had transformed into a place of fear and suspicion. Any student who dared to defy this draconian decree, the administration ominously warned, would face "summary dismissal," a chilling threat that hung heavy in the air, silencing even the most ardent voices of dissent.

A chilling irony followed the resumption of academic activities. The cultists, those very individuals who had been apprehended by university security and handed over for disciplinary action, were brazenly parading across campus. They cruised in their vehicles, a chilling display of defiance.

Rumors circulated like wildfire, whispers of threats and ominous pronouncements. The cultists, it was said, vowed to exact retribution upon the student union members who had dared to challenge their authority. A series of chilling reports surfaced, reaching the ears of the students union leaders. These reports spoke of impending attacks, of cultists plotting to invade student hostels in the dead of night. Yet, the administration, seemingly unconcerned, dismissed these warnings with a dismissive shrug. A disconcerting sense of apathy permeated the halls of power, leaving students to grapple with a growing sense of unease.

Days bled into weeks, weeks into months, and an eerie silence descended upon the campus. The vibrant pulse of student life, once a vibrant symphony of activity, was muted, replaced by a chilling stillness. Fear, a venomous serpent, slithered into the hearts of students. The once-familiar comfort of late-night study sessions in the library or classrooms was shattered, replaced by a gnawing dread of unseen assailants. The campus, once a haven of intellectual pursuit, had become a battleground, a silent theater of fear and uncertainty."

The 10th of July 1999 etched itself indelibly upon the annals of campus unionism and the turbulent history of cult clashes in Nigeria. The preceding day, a vibrant tapis of joy had unfolded within the confines of my father's rented apartment at 54 Oroona Street, Modakeke, Ile-Ife. My elder sister Toyin's traditional wedding ceremony had drawn a throng of relatives from our ancestral home in Ado Ekiti, converging to honor my father with their presence. The air thrummed with the festive spirit of the occasion, a symphony of laughter and shared blessings.

As the festivities waned, casting long shadows across the twilight, my cousin, Adeleke Omolade now a distinguished professor of Economics at the Federal University Oye Ekiti, who had journeyed from Ado to grace the occasion expressed a desire to accompany me back to the university. He yearned to experience the vibrant nocturnal pulse of OAU campus nightlife, and I, eager to share this facet of my world with him, readily agreed. We bid farewell to the revelers and embarked upon the journey towards Awo Hall, my abode within the university's hallowed grounds.

As we navigated the gateway to the hostel, a figure emerged from the shadows, George Iwilade, a luminary known to all as Afrika, the Secretary-General of the Obafemi Awolowo Student Union. A law student of exceptional intellect and unwavering conviction, Afrika was a beacon of student activism, his influence radiating beyond the university's confines and reverberating throughout the southwestern academic landscape. His spirit was indomitable, his voice a clarion call for justice and equality.

Afrika, a constant thorn in the flesh of both the university management and the ruling junta; the iron-fisted military government of the time was a figure of both legend and trepidation. Though youthful, his spirit was indomitable, his energy boundless. Adeleke, thrilled by the unexpected encounter, exchanged pleasantries with the enigmatic figure before taking his leave.

Coincidentally, that very night, the air crackled with the electric energy of the Kegites Word Conference. The Kegites, or the Palm Wine

Drinkers Club, reigned supreme among Nigerian university social clubs. Born from the fertile ground of the University of Ife (now Obafemi Awolowo University) in 1962, the club had woven itself into the very fabric of campus life.

Their unique greeting, a solemn exchange of right thumbs and index fingers was a testament to their distinctive identity. That night, the Awo Hall Cafeteria throbbed with excitement as initiates were welcomed into the fold. Visitors from every corner of the nation; north, east, and south had converged, eager to witness the ceremony and partake in the revelry

The rhythmic pulse of the Kegite gyration, a vibrant fabric woven from palm-wine-infused songs and exuberant dance, had held us captive until the wee hours. My cousin and I, weary but exhilarated, finally retreated to my sanctuary – the executive room granted to me as a member of the Hall Executive. This sanctuary, a haven for my friends, was typically a refuge from the boisterous communal life of the hostel. Unlike the cramped room shared by four students, my room was a solitary space, a privilege I cherished.

Inside, we encountered Toyin Ogunleye, my steadfast friend and classmate, already slumbering peacefully on my bed. Toyin, though residing off-campus, had sought solace and camaraderie in my room, his illness prompting him to seek the comfort of friendship. Banji, now forever silenced by the cruel hand of fate, lay peacefully asleep on the couch. With a practiced ease, I retrieved a few spare mattresses from my wardrobe, transforming the floor into a makeshift bed for my cousin and myself.

As we settled, the echoes of the night lingered; lively conversations, the rhythmic beat of distant music. But the tranquility was shattered by an unexpected intrusion. A single gunshot pierced the stillness, a jarring discordance in the nocturnal symphony of OAU. We dismissed it initially, attributing it to the exuberant revelry of the Kegite club, perhaps an errant firework. However, another shot, followed by the frantic clatter of running feet, shattered our complacency. The crescendo of gunfire, drawing ever closer, painted a stark picture of impending danger.

Panic began to grip us. Voices, guttural and menacing, echoed through the corridors: "Come out, Awo boys, come out!" then,

"Legacy, come out! We are here for you!" Lanre Legacy, the Student Union President, one of their target. Fear, cold and clammy, seized us. We were paralyzed, our bodies trembling, our minds racing. Banji urged someone to switch off the room light and silence the soft music that had been our lullaby. But fear had rendered us immobile, our limbs heavy with dread.

Then, a chilling sound – the insistent thud of a heavy object against my door. It was a determined assault, a desperate attempt to breach our sanctuary. The door, thankfully, held firm, a fragile barrier against the encroaching chaos.

The pre-dawn silence was shattered by a woman's voice, a chilling command echoing through the room: "It's time to go!" A sudden, chilling silence followed, the air thick with unspoken dread. Though we knew they had fled, a paralyzing fear gripped us. None dared to venture outside. Finally, summoning the courage of a cornered animal, I rose and cautiously opened the door. The courtyard was a scene of chaos, students huddled together in small, terrified groups.

I quickly dressed, the urgency of the situation spurring me into action. As a Hall Executive, I felt a responsibility to understand the unfolding horror. Reaching the cafeteria, I was met with a scene of carnage. Blood stained the floor, shards of glass littered the ground, a testament to the violence that had erupted.

The sight that awaited me in the Hall Chairman's room would forever be etched into my memory. Two rooms before Lema's room,

I stumbled upon a tableau of unimaginable brutality. Yemi Iwilade, affectionately known as Afrika, lay lifeless, a grotesque crimson stain blooming on the floor. His skull, shattered by a brutal blow, lay nearby, a macabre testament to the savagery of the attack. Four other students had met a similar fate.

The air was thick with the stench of blood and fear. About twenty-five others lay injured, casualties of the ensuing stampede and the indiscriminate violence. The Student Union Secretary-General, George Yemi Iwilade, a brilliant young medical student, Eviano Ekelemu, a graduating student poised on the cusp of a promising future, Yemi Ajiteru, Babatunde Oke, a budding philosopher, and Ekpede Godfrey all extinguished by the cold, calculating cruelty of their assailants. It was a day that would forever scar the university's history.

Though shattered, our spirits refused to be broken. Lanre Legacy, the Union President, rallied us, a fierce determination burning in his eyes. We embarked on a relentless pursuit of justice, utilizing our intelligence network to track down the perpetrators. In a series of daring operations, we apprehended three individuals: Aisekhaghe Aikhile, a first-year Agricultural Economics student, Emeka Ojuagu, and Frank Idahosa, known as Efosa. Efosa and Ojuagu were apprehended in a public transport vehicle, their escape attempt thwarted.

Confined to the Awolowo Hall "Coffee Room," a notorious holding cell, Efosa and Oguagu confessed to their involvement in the heinous attack. Efosa, with chilling clarity, revealed that the massacre was a calculated act of revenge, a brutal retribution for the earlier apprehension and detention of several Black Axe members within the hall.

The tragedy sent shockwaves across the nation. The Vice-Chancellor, Professor Wale Omole, was unceremoniously removed from his post by the Federal Government. A panel of inquiry was swiftly established to investigate the horrific events, a desperate attempt to bring some semblance of justice to the bereaved and to prevent such a tragedy from ever occurring again. It was a day that would forever remain etched in the annals of the university's history, a grim reminder of the fragility of life and the enduring power of human darkness.

CHAPTER FOUR
BRAIN, BEAUTY AND
CHARACTER (BBC)

The year was 2003, I found myself once again standing on the familiar grounds of Obafemi Awolowo University, this time not as an undergraduate, but as a postgraduate student. Little did I know that this second admission would not only further my academic pursuits but also fulfil a destiny that had been etched in the stars.

Ten years prior, fate had intervened, weaving together the threads of my life and Ajibike's. It was during my JAMB examination in 1994, held at Federal Government College Akure that our paths first crossed. Ajibike, then a student in SS2, might be among the group of students in their pristine green and white uniforms that welcomed us into the school premise to write my Joint Admission Matriculation Board Examination. While I couldn't be certain if she was among them, her presence within the school was undeniable.

Now, back at Great Ife, I found myself residing in Muritala Mohammed Postgraduate Students Hall Block J. My involvement in campus politics led to my appointment to the PG Planning Committee. It was during one of our initial meetings that I encountered her. Sitting across the table, Ajibike stood out, a vision of beauty amidst the crowd. Her ethereal beauty, coupled with the tales of mysterious mermaids from the nearby River Opa, left me questioning her very humanity. Could she be one of those mythical creatures, masquerading as a student?

My mind raced with a whirlwind of thoughts, unable to focus on the meeting. Love, at first sight, had struck me with an undeniable force. As the meeting drew to a close, I found myself eagerly anticipating the moment when I could finally introduce myself and take the first step towards a future that had been foretold.

It was after a PG Committee meeting that I found myself drawn to Ajibike, a quiet, unassuming postgraduate student. With a mixture of trepidation and excitement, I mustered the courage to introduce myself. To my surprise, she greeted me with a familiar smile, her response catching me off guard. "I know you," she said, her voice soft and melodic.

Intrigued, I asked how she could possibly recognize me. Her answer was both unexpected and heart-warming. "Whenever I cook dinner in my kitchenette at PG Hall, I watch you and others play football," she explained. "You're a very popular player, and your name is always echoing across the field." I had never considered the possibility that someone might be observing me from afar, let alone a beacon of beauty. The thought of my name being shouted in admiration by the crowd filled me with a sense of pride and accomplishment.

Ajibike, a devout Christian often described as an SU "Scriptural Union" type, was a stark contrast to my more outgoing and loud personality. Yet, she possessed a genuine warmth and kindness that made her instantly likable. Despite her religious beliefs, she insisted that she saw all humans as equal, regardless of their backgrounds or personality.

When I expressed my interest in becoming her boyfriend, she was hesitant. She explained that she was already engaged and that she could only see me as a mere friend. While I was disappointed, because I wanted more than a friend, I was not deterred. To me, having the most beautiful and admired postgraduate student on campus as a friend was a significant accomplishment. I agreed to her terms, and our journey began.

Our friendship started with casual conversations, shared meals (I remember vividly how she used to give me the leftovers from her refrigerator whenever she was travelling to her base in Lagos), and occasional study sessions at night in the academic area specifically at the Faculty of Social Sciences. Ajibike's gentle nature and unwavering support provided a much-needed respite from the stresses of academic life. She was always there to lend a listening ear, offer advice, or simply share a laughter. As our bond grew stronger, I began to appreciate the depth of her character. Ajibike was a woman of strong principles, guided by her faith and a deep-seated desire to make a positive impact on the world. She was passionate about Christ and relationship issues, often volunteering her time to various causes on campus. She pioneered a group of beautiful postgraduate female student fellowship.

My friendship with Ajibike made me begin to re-evaluate my own goals and aspirations. I realized that my political representation on campus could be a powerful platform for positive change. With Ajibike's encouragement and support, I became more involved in postgraduate student politics and began to advocate for issues that were important to me and my fellow students. Together, we were both involved in organizing a programme to raise awareness about social justice. We brought Jide Babalakin a renowned lawyer, a son of a judge from Gbogan to Ileife. We also worked together under the leadership of the then Chairman of Postgraduate student, Ogunleye Temitope aka RST to bring Big Sam Ebunolu Onagoruwa to Great Ife for a seminar on inclusive and equitable justice in Nigeria.

Ajibike's wisdom and guidance were invaluable, and her influence helped me to develop a stronger sense of purpose and direction. As our friendship deepened, we also faced challenges. One such test came when I contested and lost by a narrow margin the Chairmanship position of the PG Hall Executive. Ajibike's unwavering belief in me helped me to overcome obstacles and achieve my goals as a student. As we approached the end of our postgraduate studies, we knew that our paths would likely diverge. However, the bond we had formed would endure. Ajibike had become an integral part of my life, and I was grateful for the friendship we had cultivated.

Our story is a testament to the power of human connection. It is a reminder that even in the most unlikely of circumstances, friendships can blossom and have a profound impact on our lives. Ajibike's kindness, wisdom, and unwavering support had transformed me in countless ways, and I wanted more. "I've always been a hopeless romantic person. Whenever I watched movies with love stories, I couldn't help but imagine myself with a woman who was not only beautiful but also intelligent and kind. In my mind, I had already found her, but it seemed she hadn't found me yet.

I once met the love of my life, but she was already engaged and about to marry someone else. It was a heart breaking experience. I questioned why fate hadn't brought us together when she was single. Despite the disappointment, I never gave up hope. I believed that nothing was impossible for God. In November 2006, I gave my life to Christ. It was a transformative moment. I became a new person, a redeemed soul, cleansed of my sins. My faith in God grew stronger than ever. I began to believe in the unbelievable. And God never let me down. One fateful night, I had a dream, a recurring dream that often signalled significant life events. In this dream, I was flying, carrying a woman on my back. We landed in a strange place, unable to understand the language. Fear and trepidation surrounded us, but we held onto each other tightly.

When I woke up, it was a Saturday morning. My friend Prof Titilayo's tenth wedding anniversary was being celebrated in Lagos, and I was the MC. As I arrived at the venue, I spotted Ajibike among the guests. I was surprised because she hadn't mentioned coming. As I hosted the ceremony, I noticed something was off about Ajibike. She seemed radiant, but there was an underlying sadness. I remembered the dream I'd had that morning. Could she have had a similar dream? These thoughts lingered in my mind until I could speak to her.

I finally mustered the courage to ask, "Is everything alright, Ajibike? You don't seem yourself." She revealed that her fiancé had broken up with her after their traditional family introduction. My heart sank. How could anyone break up with such an incredible woman? It was a moment of profound realization. Perhaps fate had a different plan for us after all.

I told Ajibike not to be discouraged by this disappointment, that God would make everything beautiful for her in His own time. With a playful nudge, I suggested that maybe everything happened because of my unwavering interest in her. We both laughed it off, letting the disappointment fade away.

After the event, we went our separate ways. The next day, she returned home. Feeling a newfound optimism about Ajibike, I knew I needed to seek God's guidance. I craved a quiet, distraction-free environment to ask Him a simple question, to lay a simple task before Him. Redemption Camp, with its bustling activity, wouldn't suffice. So I opted for the tranquillity of Canaan Land, the Winners Chapel Ministry at Ota.

The previous weekend, before hosting my friend's wedding anniversary, I visited my good friend Akin. There, I reconnected with a few classmates from our 2000 graduation days, including Bimbo, one of the most stunning women in our class. Back in undergrad, my impoverished background prevented me from mustering the courage to even approach her. Now, eight years later, neither of us were married, and our friends, with a mischievous glint in their eyes, tried to nudge us together.

Curious about her marital status, I asked Bimbo why she remained unmarried. She confided in me the string of disappointments she'd faced in her search for a partner. The question boomeranged back to me. "Dare, why haven't you tied the knot?" she inquired. I poured out my heart, explaining my love for a woman currently entangled with another man who, sadly, didn't reciprocate her feelings.

Bimbo, a woman of unwavering encouragement, urged me to persevere. While she gently nudged me to keep pursuing Ajibike, I sensed a flicker of openness, a hint of possibility if I were to show interest. Right there, I made a solemn vow to myself. I would redouble my efforts for the woman who held my heart, Ajibike. Fuelled by my newfound faith, I was convinced that nothing was beyond God's reach. Prayer, I believed, was the key to unlocking Ajibike's heart, especially now that she was free from the constraints of her previous relationship.

Reaching Sango Ota at 8 pm, I made my way to Canaan Land. I found myself ushered into the sports arena within Covenant University, nestled amidst the vast expanse of Canaan Land. Armed with ten carefully crafted prayer points, I embarked on a ten-hour marathon of fervent supplication, from 9 pm to 6 am. Each point was meticulously aimed at opening Ajibike's eyes to see the glory God had bestowed upon me. I channelled the fervour of David's prayers, the unwavering faith of Hannah, and the resolute hope of Jesus gazing heavenward, pleading for clarity on my future wife. I poured out my heart until my voice grew hoarse, and at 6 am, I concluded my prayers, brimming with anticipation that God had heard my pleas. I departed Ota the shores of Canaan Land of Winners Chapel, buoyed by the unwavering belief that my audacious prayer had found favour in the eyes of the divine. The next step was clear: I must confess my intentions to Ajibike.

Without delay, I embarked on a journey to Ile-Ife, the following weekend. As the Yoruba proverb wisely states, *"Ohun to wu ni, nii po loro eni,"* one's heart's desire should be one's highest priority. Upon arriving in Ile-Ife, I informed Ajibike of a fabricated weekend visit to my parents, concealing my true purpose. We agreed to rendezvous at the Faculty of Social Sciences Foyer that night. I had meticulously rehearsed my lines, planning to captivate her with romantic tales and poetic verses, a common strategy employed by young lovers. I even considered invoking the divine, claiming a prophetic revelation that she was my destined partner. However, as fate would have it, my carefully constructed script crumbled upon her arrival. In that moment, stripped of eloquence and artifice, I realized that the simplest truth was the most profound. The words that flowed from my lips were raw and honest: "This is the woman I wish to spend the rest of my life with."

She arrived promptly at the appointed hour, her presence filling the foyer. A dilemma seized me: a hug or a handshake? Uncertain of the appropriate gesture, I opted for a compromise, uttering a spontaneous, "Hello, my angel." The words, unexpected even to myself, seemed to hang in the air. She responded with outstretched arms, and we embraced warmly.

Gazing into her eyes, I declared, "I have chosen you to be my wife." A moment of silence followed, then, a question: "What do you want me to say?" My reply was direct: "Just say yes." She requested time for reflection, and so, the wait continued. A weight, long borne, finally lifted. I had bared my soul to Ajibike, confessed my love, and she, though hesitant, had granted me the gift of time. With a heart both hopeful and anxious, I departed Ile-Ife for Lagos the following Monday. I placed my trust in the divine, certain that the wait would not be interminable.

Midweek, my phone rang. The caller was Professor Bukola Ojo, Ajibike's revered mentor and academic mother. She conveyed a message that surprised me. Ajibike, it seemed, had painted a different picture of her family. While she had spoken of retired parents residing in Lagos, this woman presented herself as a maternal figure. I responded with calm and respect, a natural ability honed over years of engaging with diverse individuals. When Professor Ojo requested a character reference, a name sprang to mind. Professor Titilayo Ayotunde, a senior friend and a classmate during our MSc degree, was the perfect choice. His endorsement would lend credibility to my character and intentions.

A week subsequent to my telephone conversation with Professor Bukola Ojo, she extended an invitation for a tête-à-tête in her office. The year was 2008, and my birthday 11th July was three days away. Concurrently, my bond with Ajibike, 'my angel,' as I now affectionately called her, continued to deepen. I was certain that she was a divine messenger, entrusted with a celestial message to be delivered through the sacred institution of matrimony. Our camaraderie flourished, and I was filled with hope and confidence that our journey would culminate in a blissful union.

On the tenth day of July, 2008, I found myself alone with Professor Ojo in her office. She subjected me to a series of inquiries that made it abundantly clear she had approved of me as a potential suitor for her 'daughter'. She revealed that those she had consulted about me had spoken highly of my character. However, she issued a stern warning: should I ever cause her daughter pain, I would face her wrath. With a solemn prayer for my future, she dismissed me.

On the cusp of my thirty-third year, I felt a profound readiness. The stage was set for a pivotal moment, a declaration of love that would forever alter the course of my life. I chose the hallowed ground of PG Hall, the very place where our destiny had first intertwined three years prior. As the dawn painted the sky with hues of promise, I posed the eternal question: "Would you be my wife?" Her answer, a resounding "Yes," ignited a flame of love that continues to burn brightly, a testament to the enduring power of our bond.

Ajibike's affirmative response to my proposal ignited a whirlwind of anticipation. I yearned to expedite our journey towards matrimony, eager to embark on the next chapter of our lives. Yet, fate, with its capricious hand, intervened. Few days into our courtship, Ajibike delivered a seismic revelation: a Chinese Government scholarship beckoned her to pursue a doctoral degree, necessitating a four-year sojourn to the Far East.

I was utterly dumbfounded. My heart, once filled with dreams of wedded bliss, now plummeted into a chasm of uncertainty. In the recesses of my memory, China was a distant land, a realm conjured by childhood fantasies. The martial arts prowess of Bruce Lee and Jackie Chan, the mystical allure of Shaolin Temple, these were the sole facets of Chinese culture that had imprinted themselves upon my mind. The intricate, tonal nuances of the Mandarin language, a linguistic labyrinth, had always seemed both fascinating and formidable. Now, my beloved was poised to traverse this enigmatic landscape, leaving me behind to grapple with the solitude of a long-distance love.

A tempest brewed within me. Though my heart swelled with love for Ajibike, the prospect of a four-year hiatus before our union cast a long, dark shadow. Why, I wondered, had the divine hand bestowed upon me a dream so perfect, only to then banish her to the distant shores of China? A plethora of questions echoed in my mind, each one more perplexing than the last.

Seeking solace and guidance, I turned to the heavens above. Kneeling in humble supplication, I implored the Almighty God to illuminate my path. My first course of action was to seek clarity from Ajibike herself. Without hesitation, she declared her intention to honor the admission offer. Yet, she offered a glimmer of hope, suggesting a compromise: she would return after the initial year, we would wed, and then she would depart once more to complete her studies.

I suggested to Ajibike that we hasten our traditional marriage and swiftly follow it with a Registry ceremony before her departure. Yet, she demurred, asserting her inability to broach such a proposal with her parents. As my perplexity deepened, divine guidance remained steadfast. I recalled the significance of my names: Oluwadamilare, signifying that God would always vindicate me, and Ifeoluwa, affirming that God's will would prevail. Despite the tempestuous turmoil within my mind, one truth remained immutable: I had discovered my soulmate, the missing piece of my existence, and I would not relinquish her, not even for the allure of distant land of chopsticks.

The universe, in its infinite wisdom, had woven a unique thread into the fabric of our lives. Her academic aspirations, a coveted PhD offer from a prestigious Chinese university, beckoned her across the globe. A bittersweet prospect, it threatened to separate us, yet it was a testament to her brilliance and unwavering pursuit of knowledge. After much deliberation and heartfelt prayer, I found myself yielding to the inevitable. Her dreams, as noble as they were, took precedence. The clock, however, was ticking. With a departure date looming in mid-September, we were confronted with a daunting timeline – a mere two months to navigate the complexities of love, logistics, and cultural nuances.

The first step, a crucial one, was to introduce Ajibike to the most important man in my life: my father. A revered figure, his approval was paramount. My father, ever the discerning judge of character, was immediately captivated by her intelligence and grace. He posed a series of insightful questions, each a test of her wisdom and understanding. She navigated these inquiries with poise and eloquence, leaving him thoroughly impressed.

In the days that followed, I introduced Ajibike to my two younger brothers. Their admiration for her was immediate and unwavering. They saw in her not just a beautiful woman, but a kindred spirit, a brilliant mind, and a loving soul. Their enthusiasm for our union was infectious, and it further solidified my resolve. As the days turned into weeks, a serendipitous opportunity arose. My elder sister, Toyin, a woman of unwavering strength and wisdom, journeyed from the distant lands of Sokoto to visit our father at Ile-ife. A rare occasion, indeed, given the vast expanse that separated us. I seized the moment, inviting Ajibike to meet my sister, a crucial step in solidifying our bond.

The rendezvous was a harmonious blend of tradition and modernity. As they shared a meal, ate from the same plate, their laughter echoed through the room, a symphony of shared joy. Ajibike, with her warmth and grace, effortlessly won my sister's heart. Her approval, a blessing bestowed upon our love, was a testament to the purity of our intentions. Having been introduced to my father, Sister Toyin, and my two younger brothers, it was time to acquaint Ajibike with my eldest sister, Yemisi Adeyeye who lived in Wakajaiye, Ibadan at the time. She had assumed the maternal role in our family following our mother's untimely demise in 1993. A devout Christian like our mother, Yemisi was a pillar of strength and faith.

After Ajibike's initial meeting with sister Yemisi, she contacted me later same evening, requesting specific details: her mother's information, her father's information, her hometown, and her own personal details. I provided all the requested information. Later on, as I reflected on the nature of the inquiry, I recalled scenes from Nollywood home videos where similar requests often signalled the beginning of spiritual investigation.

The following day, I called sister Yemisi to inquire about the purpose behind her request. My suspicions were confirmed: she had consulted a respected Prophetess, Mrs. Abikanlu, in Ibadan, Oyo State, renowned for her genuine spiritual guidance. Sister Yemisi shared a Yoruba proverb with me, *"Ohun to dara n fe adura, eyi ti o daa na, adura la o fi yii pada,"* which translates to, "Good things require prayers, and bad things can be rectified through fervent prayers." I expressed my unwavering commitment to Ajibike, declaring that no spiritual revelation would deter me from going forward with her. I was resolute in my decision, and I was prepared to face any challenges that might arise.

In the early days of September, I accompanied Ajibike to the residence of my sister, Yemisi, nestled in the serene neighbourhood of Wakajaiye. However, upon our arrival, sister Yemisi revealed that she had just returned from a visit with her friend, the prophetess. A divine decree had been issued, blessing our union and granting us permission to embark on the sacred journey of matrimony. Yet, a caveat accompanied this divine blessing: a gentle reminder to exercise patience and temper my fiery spirit. This sage advice has remained etched in my memory, guiding my actions to this very day. Moreover, the prophetess offered a cascade of prophecies, some of which have already unfolded, while others await their appointed time.

A Yoruba proverb, *"Eegun nla ni kehin Igbale,"* aptly describes the grand finale. The only person Ajibike had yet to encounter was my elder brother, Tayo, a distinguished barrister who worked at Globacom, Lagos, Nigeria. His lucrative position, secured a year before our firstborn, Gbenga's untimely demise, has been a lifeline for our family. As the sole provider, Tayo has selflessly shouldered the financial burdens of our extended family, from the orphaned children of our late brother to my own education and that of my younger sibling. A paragon of benevolence, Tayo's influence on my life is immeasurable. Ever striving for excellence, he inspires those around him to reach their full potential.

Having painted a vivid portrait of Tayo to Ajibike, I eagerly anticipated their meeting. Tayo, too, was delighted by my choice, going above and beyond to ensure our relationship flourished. His unwavering support and generosity were a testament to the depth of his brotherly love. When Ajibike witnessed first-hand the warmth and affection he extended to us, she was deeply impressed. Tayo blessed our union, assuring Ajibike of his commitment to our happiness and promising to stand by us through thick and thin.

Ajibike's departure from Ile-Ife for Lagos marked a significant moment. As I offered to assist with her belongings, she mentioned the prospect of introducing me to her uncle. This presented a unique opportunity, as her uncle, Professor Michael Faborode, was the esteemed Vice Chancellor of Obafemi Awolowo University. As a young, unmarried lecturer, Ajibike had the privilege of residing at the Vice Chancellor's lodge. She had already spoken highly of me to her uncle and his wife, Dr. Mrs. Faborode, who were eager to meet me. Following my introduction of Ajibike to my family, it was now my turn to be introduced to her own, beginning with the revered first family of the university community.

As I stepped through the threshold of the Vice Chancellor's lodge, a wave of nostalgia washed over me, recalling a pivotal moment in my youth. I remembered a tumultuous era, a time of student activism and fervent protest. In 1997, I had been a part of the Aluta, a vibrant movement that had led us to occupy the very same lodge, during the tenure of Professor Wale Omole.

The contrast between then and now was stark. I was no longer a fiery young protester, but a guest, welcomed with open arms. The Vice Chancellor, despite his undoubtedly busy schedule, graciously set aside time to engage with me. As we sat in his cozy sitting room, I poured my heart out, outlining our plans and aspirations. He listened intently, his expression a blend of interest and understanding. A knowing smile played on his lips as he inquired about Ajibike's father. When I confessed that we hadn't met, he offered sage advice, suggesting that it would be a prudent next step.

His wife, a gracious and warm hostess, extended a heartfelt invitation to visit their home whenever I found myself in Ile-Ife. Her hospitality was a testament to the kindness and generosity of the academic community. With the final touches completed, Ajibike's belongings were secured in the car. As we drove away from the Vice Chancellor's lodge, I couldn't help but reflect on the extraordinary journey that had led me to this moment.

In Western Nigeria, the institution of marriage transcends a mere union of two individuals. It's often a solemn contract between two families, a cultural tapestry woven with deep-rooted traditions. The Yoruba people, with their rich heritage, exemplify this familial emphasis. This intricate social fabric can undoubtedly complicate divorce, as the dissolution of a marriage is perceived as a rupture not just between two individuals but between two families.

My journey into this cultural nuance began when I introduced Ajibike to my family. The warm reception I received solidified my belief in the strength of our bond, Ajibike was eager to reciprocate by seeking the blessing of her family in Lagos. As I sat in the opulent living room of the Lawani family home in Apapa, Lagos, I was filled with a mix of anticipation and reverence. The room, adorned with Western-style furnishings, exuded a sense of prosperity and sophistication.

Mr. Foluso Lawani, a retired public servant and my future father-in-law, presided over the meeting. His opening prayer, a lengthy invocation, was delivered with the gravitas of a seasoned orator. His wife, Mrs. Cecilia Lawani, and their eldest daughter, Mrs. Jumoke Adams, who had recently given birth, completed the gathering. I had already been warmly welcomed by Mrs. Adams during a previous visit to her home in Surulere. Her acceptance had given me hope, and I was eager to win over the hearts of the rest of the family. The meeting was like an interview for a job. My future father-in-law posed a question akin to a university entrance exam: "Introduce yourself and explain why you've chosen to marry my daughter."

I managed to articulate a simple, sincere response. He then surprised me, questioning if I had met Ajibike's godfather, Mr. Laoye Jaiyeola. When I confessed I have not, he emphasized the deep-rooted connection between the two families and hinted at a rigorous screening process awaiting me. It felt as though I was applying for a top job, but I pressed on, determined to navigate this unexpected challenge. Her mother, Mrs

Lawani, a devout and perceptive woman, observed me quietly throughout the encounter.

The meeting concluded on a positive note, with a delicious meal of rice, fish, and beef stew. As I departed with my fiancée, we headed to the Jaiyeola residence in Oduduwa, Apapa. Mr. Laoye Jaiyeola, a distinguished banker and a pillar of his church community, welcomed me into his opulent Apapa residence with a warmth that belied his formidable reputation. His wife, a gracious and refined woman, complemented his hospitality, and their children, Tomi, Ibukun, and the precocious Fikayo, radiated joy. The home, a testament to their success, was clearly a second home to Ajibike.

Mr. Jaiyeola engaged me in a series of insightful questions, his interest extending beyond the present to the future. He inquired about my support for Ajibike's academic aspirations, her dream of becoming a university professor. I assured him of my unwavering commitment to her goals. With a satisfied nod, he bestowed his blessing upon our relationship, welcoming me into the family fold.

As the day of Ajibike's departure for China approached, a whirlwind of emotions and logistical challenges threatened to overwhelm us. Yet, on September 12, 2008, I stood at the Muritala Mohammed International Airport, watching as her Southern China Airways flight soared into the sky. For the next one year, distance would test our bond, but our faith in God and our shared dreams sustained us. We yearned for her return, ten months later, when we would finally unite in marriage.

On the 30th June, 2009, Ajibike's return from the distant shores of China marked the countdown to our nuptials, scheduled for the 18th of July, a week shy of my 34th birthday. I had initially envisioned myself in a pristine white suit, a classic symbol of purity. But wiser counsel prevailed, and I opted for a refined grey ensemble, complemented by a crisp cream shirt and a dash of color in a pink tie.

My younger brother, a loyal companion, had graciously accepted the role of best man. Ajibike, ever thoughtful, had chosen her 'younger sister', Tomi Jaiyeola, to be her chief bridesmaid. The stage was set, the players were ready. The reunion with my angel, after ten long months of transcontinental longing, was a moment of pure joy. Despite the physical distance, our bond had been nurtured through countless hours of digital communion. My humble abode had transformed into a virtual sanctuary, a space where our souls converged across the miles.

To prepare for our future together, we embarked on marriage counseling sessions. These insightful discussions provided us with invaluable tools and perspectives to navigate the complexities of married life. The counselor's guidance and the unwavering support of our families were instrumental in solidifying our bond.

Ajibike's family, particularly her elder sister, Mrs. Jumoke Adams, played a pivotal role in the wedding preparations. Her meticulous attention to detail, especially in curating our attire, was commendable. Her brothers, Jide and Odun, were equally supportive, contributing to the overall festive atmosphere.

As the 18th of July approached, Ajibike and I embarked on a three-day fast, a Christian tradition known in Yoruba language as "*biribiri*." While fasting was not my forte, I relied on divine intervention to endure the rigorous spiritual exercise. It was tough but God saw us through. On the final day, we sought solace in the quietude of the Redemption Camp, entrusting our wedding and future to the divine plan.

July 18, 2009, marked a momentous day as we exchanged vows at the historic St. George Military Church in Apapa. The sacred grounds of the church hosted not only the traditional wedding ceremony but also the grand reception. Guests from across Nigeria and even overseas graced the occasion, including dignitaries and prominent figures from various walks of life. The catering service was impeccable, ensuring that every guest was well-fed and satisfied. I was particularly touched by the presence of my childhood friends from CAC Ondo Road Modakeke Ile-Ife, as well as my classmates from Aquinas and Oyemekun Grammar School. The OAU Pensioners' Association and university staff also showed their support in significant numbers. It was truly an unforgettable event filled with joy and celebration. Immediately after the reception, we embarked on a week-long honeymoon at the Covenant Ground of Winners Chapel in Ota.

As we reflect on our journey, we recognize the invaluable role that God has played in our marriage. His unwavering presence has been a constant source of strength and guidance, nurturing our love and ensuring the enduring blossom of our union.

CHAPTER FIVE
A FLIGHT OF FANTASY: FROM CHILDHOOD DREAMS TO REALITY

The dream had haunted me since childhood, a vivid, recurring vision of soaring through the night sky, my wings unfurling like those of a bird. It was a fantasy born of innocence, a child's escape from the mundane, a testament to the boundless imagination that fuels our youthful dreams.

The first time I remember experiencing this dream, I was around nine years old in primary four at Christ Apostolic Church Elementary

School at Oke-Aanu, Ondo Road, Modakeke, Ile-ife, Osun State Nigeria. In it, I found myself flying over a bustling town of Ile-ife, a town believed to be the source of all Yoruba people worldwide and the cradle of the universe where all humanity started, the cacophony of voices and sounds rising up to meet me. The buildings below were towering structures of stone and brick, their windows glowing with a warm, inviting light. The streets were teeming with people, their faces a blur of colour and movement.

As I soared higher, the city began to shrink beneath me, revealing a vast, sprawling landscape. Forests stretched out as far as the eye could see, their emerald green leaves shimmering in the sunlight. Rivers wound their way through the countryside, reflecting the clear blue sky above. Fear crept into my dream as I realized that I was alone, adrift in a world that was both familiar and utterly foreign. I tried to call out for help, but my voice was lost in the wind. The people below stared up at me, their eyes wide with astonishment and perhaps a hint of unease. They pointed and gestured, but I couldn't understand a word they were saying.

As I grew older, the dream continued to visit me, its details evolving and expanding. Sometimes, I would fly to distant lands, exploring exotic landscapes and encountering mythical creatures. Other times, I would soar high above the clouds, feeling a sense of freedom and exhilaration that I had never known in waking life.

Whenever I shared these dreams with adults, their reactions were often mixed. Some dismissed them as mere flights of fancy, while others expressed concern that I might be delving into the realm of the supernatural. One spiritual man in 'Alekuwodo Oshogbo' even suggested that I was destined for great things, that I would one day travel to the ends of the earth.

In 2009, the dream of a lifetime was about to become a reality. I was finally going to leave my native Nigeria and join my wife in China, the land of chopsticks. The anticipation was palpable, a mix of excitement and trepidation. As I prepared to depart, a sense of déjà vu washed over me. It was as if I had been preparing for this moment my entire life. I had always felt a deep connection to the world beyond my own, a yearning to explore the unknown. Now, that yearning was about to be fulfilled.

The morning of my departure was a blur of activity. My father, father-in-law, mother-in-law, elder brother, and his wife all accompanied me to the airport. As I checked in, I couldn't help but feel a pang of nostalgia. This was a momentous occasion, a turning point in my life.

As I was about to proceed to the boarding gate, my father, in his usual characteristic fashion, suggested that we pray. I knew what was coming and tried to pre-empt him, hoping to avoid a public spectacle. But to no avail, he insisted, and before I knew it, he had asked me to kneel down in the middle of the busy airport, offering up prayers for my safe journey and favour in a strange land. I was mortified, although this was not my first time leaving Nigeria, having travelled to Ghana and the Republic of Benin, this was my first intercontinental trip, a journey of fourteen long hours. I didn't want to draw any unnecessary attention to myself.

As my family members took turns praying, I closed my eyes and silently pleaded with God to hurry them along. Finally, the prayers came to an end, and I was able to make my way to the boarding gate. As I boarded the plane, I couldn't shake the feeling that this was more than just a relocation. It was the culmination of a dream that had been with me for so long. As the plane took off, I looked out the window and saw the city below shrink into a tiny speck. It was then that I realized that my childhood fantasy had become a reality. I was finally flying into a strange land, just like I had always dreamed of doing.

Earlier on, at the Chinese embassy in Abuja, Nigeria, I had encountered a friendly man named Nicky. As I waited to collect my visa, he approached me, his face beaming with excitement. We exchanged pleasantries, and he casually asked which province I was traveling to. When I replied, "Jilin," his eyes lit up. "That's incredible!" he exclaimed. "I'm going to Jilin too. It's my first time in China, and I don't know anyone there." I assured him that my wife was already settled in Jilin, and we could perhaps travel together. The idea appealed to both of us, and we agreed to purchase our flight tickets jointly.

As we prepared for our trip, Nicky revealed that he planned to travel light, carrying only a small amount of luggage. This was good news for me, as it meant I could utilize his luggage allowance to bring along extra items. Given the long distance and the potential for food shortages, I decided to pack a variety of Nigerian staples, including garri, beans, amala, and dried fish.

The flight to China was long, but Nikky's company made the journey enjoyable. I had initially been concerned about the prospect of traveling alone, but his presence alleviated my fears. Thanks to my wife's brief language lessons, I was able to communicate basic phrases like "I love you" and "I want this" in Chinese. This simple vocabulary proved invaluable, as it allowed me to interact with the flight attendants and request additional food, snacks, drinks, and even liquor.

As we approached our destination, my mind raced with anticipation. I had been away from my wife for three months, and I couldn't wait to see her. She had been six weeks pregnant when she left, and I was eager to witness the subtle changes in her appearance. I imagined the emotional reunion at the airport, the overwhelming joy and relief of being reunited with the love of my life. I knew it would be a moment I would cherish forever.

CHANGCHUN, JILIN PROVINCE, CHINA (2008-2014)

The plane descended, its wheels kissing the icy runway of Changchun Longjia International Airport. A chill wind whipped through the terminal, a stark contrast to the tropical warmth I'd left behind. Yet, there was a certain allure to this unfamiliar city, a promise of adventure and a new chapter in my life.

Changchun, a name derived from "long" and "spring," presented a fascinating paradox. Despite its reputation as one of China's coldest cities, with winters that lasted for nearly eight months, there was a vibrant energy that pulsed through its veins. The city's history, shaped by the Chinese Eastern Railway and the Japanese occupation, had left an indelible mark on its character.

My new life in Changchun began with a whirlwind of excitement. My wife, eager to make my arrival unforgettable, had arranged for a stay at the prestigious Dahwa International Hotel on Zhiohou Dalu. This three-star hotel was a stark contrast to the bustling Nigerian atmosphere I was accustomed to. The hotel's plush red carpets and elegant decor immediately made me feel like a VIP.

My wife's thoughtful touch was evident in the familiar comfort she had prepared for me. A delicious spread of Jollof rice, fried rice, fried fish, and tender chicken awaited my arrival, a nostalgic reminder of home. After a heartfelt prayer and a refreshing shower, we shared a delightful meal together. Despite my weariness, the warmth of my wife's company kept me awake well into the night. Our conversations, laughter, and shared affection made it an evening I will cherish forever. The chill of the Chinese night was no match for the comfort of her presence and the warmth of our shared love.

In the morning, sun painted the sky in hues of gold and pink as we finally stirred from our sleep. It was well past midday, a testament to the exhaustion that had settled upon us after our long night of reunion. As we prepared to embark on our new adventure, a wave of excitement and anticipation washed over me. Today, I will venture into the heart of our new home – the university campus. My wife had been here for a year, forging friendships with people from different countries and cultures. I was eager to meet her newfound circle and immerse myself in the vibrant tapestry of cultures that had woven itself around her.

As we boarded bus 227 right in front of the hotel, the gentle sway of the bus seemed to promise a journey filled with discovery and wonder. The university campus, with its sprawling grounds and modern architecture, was a stark contrast to the campuses from my country, a completely different scenario. As we stepped onto our building Liuxuesheng Gongyou, I couldn't help but feel a surge of pride. Not only had my wife found her place here, but I too had been accepted as a postgraduate student. This was a new chapter in our lives, a chance to explore new horizons and grow together.

The Nigerian team, led by the charismatic trio of Rebecca Agboola, Grace Egbuonu, and Ozilichukwu Umejiakwu, received us with open arms and excitement. Their infectious laughter and warm hospitality immediately put me at ease. It was as if I had known them for years. I was also introduced to Auntie Judith and a host of other friendly faces who quickly became our surrogate family.

The following Sunday, we attended Onurri Mosaic Church, a Korean church that offered English services for foreigners. As we walked through the doors, we were greeted by a welcoming atmosphere and a diverse congregation from different countries of World except China because the law forbid them to worship with foreigners. To my surprise, my wife and six others were ordained Deacons and Deaconesses that day. It was a momentous occasion, filled with joy and celebration. I was honoured to witness such a significant milestone in their lives.

After the service, I was publicly introduced to the congregation. Their prayers and blessings warmed my heart, and I felt a deep sense of belonging. It was clear that Jbk, as they affectionately called my wife, had made a lasting impression on the community. The pastor of the church, a renowned South African missionary named Pastor William Bosch, exuded a charismatic presence. His assistant, Pastor Xavier Lynch, a gentle and soft-spoken immigrant from New Zealand, was equally welcoming. He had lived in the city for over a decade with his wife and five children, and his love for the community was evident. After the service, I met the Great Efem Ubi from Cross River in Nigeria with his amiable wife Constance, I met Sebastian from Uganda, Kwesi from Ghana, Bontsi from Botswana, and the French group led by Brother Bessan from Guinea.

Mosaic Church was more than just a place of worship; it was a vibrant community that offered a sense of belonging and support. After every Sunday service, the church members would gather for a sumptuous dinner featuring an array of dumplings, fruits, cakes, and juices. It was a tradition that we eagerly looked forward to each week.

MADE IN NIGERIA, BORN IN CHINA

As the days turned into week, I began to settle into my new life in Changchun. One of the first major tasks on my to-do list was to accompany my wife for her antenatal registration at a local hospital. I had initially encourage her to do this alone while i was still in Nigeria but she insisted that until I join her. We were eager to experience this special moment together. After careful research, we decided on a hospital that had been recommended by our Tanzanian friend, Sarah Chiwamba. She had heard positive reviews from a Rwandan friend who had given birth there.

As we stepped into the hospital, a mix of anticipation and nervousness filled the air. The first scan was a surreal experience. There, on the screen, was our tiny little life, swimming and kicking with boundless energy. It was a moment of pure joy and wonder. As I watched our baby girl develop within her mother's womb, I couldn't help but feel a deep sense of love and gratitude. I looked forward to the day when I would hold her in my arms and watch her grow into a beautiful and intelligent young woman.

The pregnancy progressed swiftly, each passing day bringing us closer to the anticipated arrival of our baby girl. We had meticulously prepared for her arrival, purchasing everything necessary to welcome her into the world. With hearts full of anticipation, we had also chosen a beautiful name for our little one.

One afternoon, while exploring the vibrant Zhongdong Market, I stumbled upon a sight that captured my heart: a colossal pink teddy bear, nearly as tall as myself. It was the largest teddy I had ever seen, and I knew instantly that it was destined to become a cherished companion for our daughter. I approached the seller and expressed my intention to purchase it for her once she was born.

As the due date approached, a sense of excitement and apprehension filled the air. Two weeks before the big day, the hospital management invited us for a meeting where they advised us that a C-section would be the safest option for both my wife and our baby. They explained that a fibroid she had could potentially complicate a natural delivery, outlining the potential risks involved. Ultimately, the decision was ours to make.

After careful consideration and seeking divine guidance through prayer, we decided to follow the doctors' advice. We chose the 6th of April as the delivery date, a special day that coincided with my mother-in-law's birthday. We felt it would be a beautiful way to connect our baby with her grandmother from the very beginning.

On the 5th of April, 2010, we packed our bags and headed to the hospital, my wife's growing belly a testament to the miracle of life within her. I often joked that her belly was the largest in all of China, a playful exaggeration that belied the profound joy and anticipation we were experiencing. We spent the night at the hospital, eager to welcome our bundle of joy.

The following morning, at around 10:00 AM, we were informed that the procedure would involve both the delivery of our baby and the removal of the fibroid. Despite my limited

Mandarin skills, I managed to communicate my concern about the duration of the process. The only information I received was a vague estimate of 30 minutes.

At 11:25 AM, our precious baby girl was brought into the world. She was a beautiful sight, crying loudly as she entered the world. I kissed her forehead, blessing her with all my love. We had chosen the name Ooreofeoluwa meaning "God's unlimited grace" for her, a name that reflected our hopes and dreams for her future. While our daughter was taken to the nursery, I remained in the theatre's reception area, anxiously awaiting my wife's return. After what felt like an eternity, a nurse emerged from the operating room. Unable to understand her words, I became increasingly worried. Could something have happened to my wife? I began to pray fervently, pleading with God to protect her.

A few minutes later, a male doctor appeared, and I approached him with a sense of urgency. I demanded to know the status of my wife, my voice filled with desperation. He spoke in Mandarin, but I refused to back down. I grabbed his arm, my patience wearing thin, and insisted that he provide me with an update. He eventually realized the need for an interpreter and brought in a woman who explained that the procedure had been more complex than anticipated but that my wife would be out soon. Relieved to hear this, I agreed to go and see my daughter in the ward, where my wife would join us shortly.

News of our baby's arrival spread quickly through the university and our church communities. Foreigners from nearly a hundred countries visited us, bringing gifts for our new born. In a moment of joy and gratitude, I ran to the shop and purchased the giant teddy bear I had seen earlier, a tangible symbol of our love for our daughter.

Her arrival marked a profound transformation in our lives, elevating us to the cherished status of "daddy and mummy." We were eternally grateful for God's blessings and the miracle of new life that had entered our world. Upon our discharge from the hospital, we eagerly awaited the arrival of my mother-in-law from Nigeria. Her presence would be invaluable as we navigated the early days of parenthood. Our first day at home was a whirlwind of emotions as we adjusted to our new roles as parents.

Bathing our new born daughter was a daunting task for both my wife and I, as we were complete novices in the art of infant care. Fortunately, we turned to the wisdom of YouTube, where we found helpful videos that guided us through the process. With the help of these online tutorials, we were able to give our daughter her first thorough bath with confidence.

On the eighth day after her birth, we celebrated our daughter's christening ceremony. The event was a joyous occasion attended by over fifty people from diverse backgrounds. Pastor Bosch, the kind and compassionate pastor who had named our daughter, performed a special ritual. He wrote a heartfelt letter, sealed it in a red envelope, and entrusted us with the task of giving it to our daughter when she turned ten.

We carefully preserved the letter, cherishing the mystery it held. On the 6th of April 2020, as our daughter celebrated her tenth birthday, we finally opened the envelope. The letter contained words of wisdom, encouragement, and blessings from Pastor Bosch. Overwhelmed with emotion, we contacted him to express our gratitude and to request his blessings for our daughter. He was delighted to offer his prayers and well wishes.

One of the most memorable aspects of my time in Changchun was the kindness and hospitality of its people. The locals were incredibly welcoming, always willing to offer directions, recommendations, or simply a friendly smile. I was particularly touched by their generosity, which extended beyond mere acts of kindness.

I recall one instance when I was struggling to communicate with a shopkeeper. Despite the language barrier, the shopkeeper went out of her way to understand my request and help me find what I was looking for. It was a small gesture, but it spoke volumes about the character of the people of Changchun. As the days turned into weeks, I began to settle into my new life in Changchun. I enrolled in language classes, explored the city's vibrant food scene, and discovered hidden gems like the Old Changchun Street, a pedestrian mall lined with traditional shops and restaurants at Guiling Lu.

I also had the opportunity to connect with other foreigners living in the city, many of whom were students at local universities. We formed a tight-knit community, sharing experiences and supporting one another as we adapted to our new surroundings. My six years in Changchun were filled with unforgettable experiences. I witnessed the city's transformation as it continued to grow and evolve. I formed lasting friendships with the locals, who became like family to me. And I discovered a city that was far more than just a cold place on a map.

Changchun was a city of endless possibilities, a place where I could explore my passions, challenge myself, and find a sense of belonging. It was a city that had captured my heart and would forever hold a special place in my memory. It was a city where my child Ooreofeoluwa was born.

As Ooreofe flourished, our academic pursuits also bore fruit. In July 2012, my wife triumphantly completed her doctoral studies, a momentous achievement that filled our hearts with pride and anticipation. With a renewed sense of purpose, we made the momentous decision to return to our homeland, Nigeria. Two months later, I embarked on a journey back to China, eager to complete my own postgraduate program which was poised to finish in 2014.

Between 2012 and 2014, a period punctuated by the rhythms of the academic calendar, I made a pilgrimage back to Nigeria during every holiday break. These journeys, though fraught with the inevitable financial burden of long-distance travel, were an essential pilgrimage, a necessary sacrifice to ensure my presence in my daughter's nascent life. I could not bear the thought of being an absentee father, a ghost hovering on the periphery of her childhood. However, as I prepared to return to

China after a blissful winter holiday spent with my family, fate intervened with a dramatic twist. On the very day I was to depart, an unforeseen event transpired, altering the course of my destiny in ways I could not have imagined. This harrowing experience, a close brush with mortality, will be recounted in detail in a later chapter.

CHAPTER SIX
LIFE AND TIME OF GBENGA:
THE FIRE CRACKER

The joy of every parent is never to see the grave of the child. There is a particular saying in Yoruba that *"Iye omo ti akara ba ko wo epo ni ko jade"* meaning it's the same quantity of beans ball that are put inside the hot fry pan that must surely come out of it. I write this piece with pains and agony in my heart because of the harrowing experience of losing our big brother, the first son of my father at the age of forty to a ghastly motor accident.

In August 1963, the same year that my parents got married, they were blessed with their first child, a bouncing baby boy. They named him so well that all the names they gave him paved way for the destiny and the future of my parents and family. They named him Oluwagbemiga (God has promoted and uplifted me) Ayodeji (My joy has become double) Victor. He can indeed be described as the son of my parents youth. My father was 24 while my mother was 20 when they both became parents.

Gbenga started school at St Andrews Primary School Oke Ila at the age of five. He was described as extremely brilliant and exceptional for his age. At the age of twelve, he was admitted to Ado Grammar School boarding house. It was a big surprise to us, his siblings, later in life how my poor parents could afford sending a child to a boarding house in those days. His exceptional talent and brain made him the pride of the school. His House-mistress, who later became a Professor at Obafemi Awolowo University Ile-ife, once described him as the exceptional kid of his time. At Ado Grammar School, his circle of friends among who are; his name's sake Gbenga Olatunji (now a pastor in New York), Gbenga Ogunsakin (late), and Prince Rufus Oyebanji (Oyee).

He worked briefly between 1981 and 1984 at the Senate Building of the University of Ife with the Principal Assistant Registrar PAR Examinations and Records. He sacrificed entering into the university to support his parent who were struggling to take care of other children. I remember vividly, how he handed over his first salary to our parents. He agreed with my parent on the sharing formula for the salary. He took a quarter of it and gave the remaining 75% to buy a commercial grinding machine for our mother. This gesture made a huge difference in the financial situation of the family.

In September 1984, Gbenga secured a place in the Department of Physical and Health Education at the esteemed University of Ife in South-western Nigeria. His initial aspiration was to study Law, but he fell short of the required admission cut-off. During that era, a missed opportunity in the Joint Admissions and Matriculation Board (JAMB) examination cut-off could be mitigated by enrolling in any available course and subsequently transferring to the desired field at the beginning of the Second year, provided a strong academic record was maintained.

Gbenga approached his studies with unwavering dedication, aiming to achieve a high grade point average that would enable him to transition into the Faculty of Law. At the conclusion of his first year, his efforts were rewarded with the highest cumulative grade among all the students of the Faculty of Education. He had acquired the necessary paperwork to change his course and had received preliminary approval from the Law Faculty.

The anticipation and joy surrounding his imminent transfer were palpable. However, an unexpected obstacle arose, the Dean of the Faculty of Education at the time, Professor Adaralegbe, adamantly refused to release Gbenga, deeming him an invaluable asset to the Faculty. Despite all interventions, the Dean remained resolute in his stance, emphasizing the importance of retaining the faculty's top student. This unfortunate turn of events dashed my elder brother's dream of studying law.

In his second year, rather than succumbing to the despondency of being denied admission to the Law program, he girded his loins and persevered in his academic pursuits. During this time, he represented his university at one of the Nigerian University Games (NUGA). Triumphantly, he emerged as the gold medallist. His achievement was met with resounding acclaim from both the university community and his family; his siblings were brimming with pride for their illustrious brother.

In the third year, a pivotal event transpired that would forever alter the trajectory of his life. The precise circumstances that led him to join the Pirate Confraternity, also known as the Seadogs, remain shrouded in mystery, though he did share with me the harrowing ordeal of the initiation process. The National Association of Seadogs, popularly known as the Pirate Confraternity, is a confraternity organization in Nigeria that is nominally University-based. The group was founded by Professor Wole Soyinka a renowned Nigerian scholar and Nobel laureate at University of Ibadan in 1952 to support human rights and social justice in Nigeria. It gained prominence during the early 1960s to late 1970s before degenerating into a clandestine and violent cult society on Nigerian campuses.

Those who found themselves drawn to membership were often individuals with an insatiable desire for power and influence within the academic milieu. While I did not perceive my brother as a power-hungry individual, I recognized that his towering stature and striking appearance may have made him a target for recruitment.

Gbenga's academic triumph in 1988 marked a historic moment for the Anuodo dynasty and our entire community. His graduation ceremony, a first for our kindred, drew extended family members from distant Ado Ekiti, who traversed a three-hour journey to witness this momentous occasion. As the graduation ceremony unfolded, a palpable sense of pride and hope filled the air. Parents, inspired by Gbenga's achievement, envisioned a brighter future for their children.

The news of his graduation from the prestigious University of Ife rippled through the town, igniting a fervent desire for education among the youth. Even those who had previously been skeptical of Western education were persuaded to encourage their children to pursue higher learning. A father in Oke-Ila famously declared, "Gbenga has no two heads; my son too can achieve greatness." Gbenga's academic excellence catalyzed a transformative shift in our community's educational aspirations.

Gbenga's academic excellence led him to an auspicious opportunity. His uncle, Dr. Yemi Ogunbiyi, a prominent figure and a friend of Nobel Laureate Wole Soyinka extended an invitation for Gbenga to come to his Ikoyi home in lagos. Dr. Ogunbiyi, then the Managing Director of Daily Times, was deeply connected to the Nigerian government. As the Federal Government, under the leadership of General Ibrahim Babangida, established the

Federal Road Safety Corps, Professor Soyinka was appointed its inaugural Corps Marshal.

Dr. Ogunbiyi, with the intention of fostering Gbenga's career, introduced him to his esteemed friend, Professor Soyinka. A sumptuous dinner had been prepared by Aunty Sade Ogunbiyi, a prelude to a memorable evening with the renowned literary figure. As Gbenga quietly dined in a corner, his adept use of Western cutlery to consume the traditional Nigerian meal of pounded yam caught Professor Soyinka's discerning eye. Intrigued, the professor inquired about the young man's identity. Dr. Ogunbiyi, proud of his wife's nephew's academic achievements and fraternal affiliations, revealed that Gbenga was a top graduate from the University of Ife and a member of the prestigious Pirate Confraternity.

Recognizing Gbenga's potential, Professor Soyinka invited him to submit his Curriculum Vitae. The subsequent rigorous interview and physical examination proved to be a stepping stone to a promising future. Gbenga was successfully commissioned as an officer in the Federal Road Safety Commission (FRSC).

Gbenga's career trajectory within the FRSC was marked by rapid advancement. He ascended to the position of Head of Operations and was deployed to various stations across the country. His postings included Ilorin, Kwara State; Suleja, Niger State; Birnin Kebbi, Kebbi State; and Benin City, Edo State. During these years, he forged lasting friendships with distinguished individuals such as Commanders Scot Olaniran, Salami, Familoni, as well as Mr. Ajayi and Dr. Nnwachuku. For a decade, Gbenga dedicated himself to supporting his father's efforts in educating his siblings, demonstrating a profound sense of familial responsibility.

Gbenga, a man of striking stature and undeniable charm, had a history of romantic pursuits before finally finding solace in the embrace of his beloved Bolanle Ogunnaike. His charm, coupled with a promising career, made him a sought-after companion. It was in the bustling city of Ilorin, during the early 1990s, that fate intervened. There, amidst the academic corridors of the prestigious Kwara Polytechnic, he encountered the ethereal Bolanle.

A spark ignited, a love at first sight that transcended superficialities. Bolanle, a gentle soul with a radiant beauty, was the antithesis of Gbenga's boisterous personality. Hailing from the serene Ijebu area of Ogun State, she had been nurtured in the cultural drapery of Oshogbo, the vibrant capital of Osun State. Recognizing the divine nature of their connection, Gbenga wasted no time in introducing Bolanle to his parents, who yearned for the establishment of his own family. Driven by a profound sense of filial duty, Gbenga prioritized the support of his parents and siblings, delaying his own marital aspirations.

In the year of 1997, their love culminated in a sacred union at the Redeemed Christian Church of God in Oshogbo. Their marriage, a beacon of love and devotion, served as an inspiration to countless young hearts around them. Four exquisite daughters, Godsmercy (born in 1998), Godslove (born in 2001), Godsfavour (born in 2003), and Godsgrace (born in 2004), were the fruits of their enduring love.

In December of 2002, upon my return from the mandatory National Youth Service Corps, Broda Gbenga as I fondly called him, urged me to embark on a Master's degree without delay. Though hesitant, I eventually yielded to his unwavering belief in my potential.

Fast forward to December 2003, I visited him for a few days in his Benin residence, as we sat together inside his compound under the moonlight, a profound conversation unfolded. He spoke of the immense potential he saw in me and my siblings, lamenting the constraints of his birth order (firstborn). He expressed his unwavering confidence in our ability to surpass his own achievements.

In return, I assured him of our admiration for his unwavering support and expressed our belief in his future greatness. As the night drew to a close, he shared his ambitious plans to purchase land in our hometown of Ado Ekiti and construct a family home. However, a chilling statement cast a shadow over our conversation. He revealed his desire to be laid to rest on this new land rather than in our ancestral family house. I dismissed his sombre prediction, assuring him of his longevity. Yet, his words, though spoken lightly, would prove to be a haunting prophecy.

On the first day of May 2004, my brother was set to attend the wedding of Commander Ajaiyi's son in Kogi State. Despite the Commander's transfer from Benin Command, my brother remained steadfast in his commitment to the event. A group of loyal officers, including my brother, planned to travel together in an official FRSC vehicle.

As the fateful morning dawned, a series of unfortunate incidents began to unfold. A minor mishap with an iron delayed my brother's departure, and a dropped mobile phone further disrupted his preparations. As he bent to retrieve the phone, he uttered a poignant remark, "Why is everything working against my attendance at this event?" Little did he know that these words would foreshadow the tragic turn of events that lay ahead.

Gbenga, while in Birnin Kebbi, one of his postings as FRSC officer gave his life to Christ. His story was similar to Saul becoming Paul in the Bible. He was a high energy person who used all his energy for the furtherance of the gospel of Christ. A dedicated Parish Pastor of the Redeemed Christian Church of God in Benin.

He arrived at his office promptly at 6:30 AM on the D-day, 1st May, 2004, half an hour ahead of the scheduled 7 AM. The following day, Sunday, was a significant day for his congregation, and he was committed to ensuring a seamless service. As he wouldn't return until the evening from a wedding event, he took the initiative to prepare the Bible study pamphlets he had already printed. With meticulous care, he arranged and collated them, sealing them in an envelope and securing them in his car.

Before embarking on his journey, Gbenga inspected the jeep that would transport them to the event. He noticed a deflated spare tire, a minor inconvenience that could derail their plans. Rather than wasting precious time, he opted for a practical solution, instructing the driver to retrieve the spare tire from his Volvo, a compatible replacement. At precisely 7 AM, they departed from Benin, their spirits high and their anticipation palpable. The event unfolded smoothly, yet an undercurrent of unease seemed to pervade Gbenga's demeanour. A junior officer observed that his mind was elsewhere, preoccupied with the impending return journey at 3 PM.

As the appointed time arrived, they paused for a group photograph, a fleeting moment captured before their tragic fate. They boarded the jeep and set off, the road stretching out before them. The initial optimism soon turned to horror as a catastrophic tire blowout around a small town called Irua, sent the vehicle careening out of control. A second tire ruptured, and the jeep somersaulted violently.

In the aftermath of the accident, a chilling silence descended. A few individuals, miraculously sustaining minor injuries, managed to extricate themselves from the wreckage. However, Gbenga, a towering figure of six foot three, lay motionless, blood seeping from a grievous head wound. Emergency services arrived, but it was too late. The once vibrant and dedicated pastor had succumbed to his injuries. At Benin Teaching Hospital, the devastating news was delivered: Gbenga had departed this earthly realm.

The next day, Sunday 2nd May, 2014, as I sat within the familiar confines of Tosin Agbelusi's abode in the serene outskirts of

Lagos, little did I know that a tempest was brewing, a storm that would irrevocably alter the course of my life. The day, seemingly ordinary, was soon to be etched in my memory as a harbinger of sorrow. As the sun began its descent, casting long shadows across the land, my friend received a phone call from my elder brother, Tayo. A lawyer of considerable repute, Tayo was then employed by the telecommunications giant, Globacom. He told my friend that I need to come and see him urgently.

I arrived at Farayola Street, Ketu Alapere where he resided. On sighting me, his voice, heavy with grief, conveyed a message that would forever scar my heart. Our beloved brother Gbenga, a beacon of hope and a pillar of strength, had been tragically snatched away from us. A wave of disbelief washed over me as I listened to Tayo relay the devastating news.

My mind raced, grappling to comprehend the cruel twist of fate. The once vibrant and promising life of my brother had been extinguished, leaving behind a void that could never be filled. The weight of the impending task fell upon my shoulders. Tayo, burdened by his professional commitments, entrusted me with the harrowing duty of travelling to Ile-ife that evening, to break the news to our father.

The journey to Ile-Ife, a pilgrimage of sorrow, lay before me. As I embarked on this mournful odyssey, the darkness of the night mirrored the despair within my soul. I sat down quietly inside the 18-seater bus and cried and cried, sobbing in agony till I reached my destination. As I sat within the confines of the bus, my mind raced like a tempestuous storm. The weight of the news pressed down on me, a heavy burden I carried alone.: how could I possibly convey such devastating news to my father? How could I break the news of my brother's untimely death without inflicting irreparable harm upon his fragile heart? I knew I couldn't simply blurt out the truth; I had to find a way to soften the blow, to prepare him for the inevitable.

I resolved to seek solace and counsel from a trusted confidant, Professor Ishola Olomola, my father's closest friend and a distinguished historian at Obafemi Awolowo University. I knew that the news would shatter his world, but I also knew that his wisdom and empathy would guide me through this harrowing ordeal.

I alighted from the bus at the university gate, my heart heavy with grief. The journey to Professor Olomola's Road 12 residence was a somber pilgrimage, a solitary walk through the fading twilight. Upon reaching his doorstep, I was greeted by his wife, who was visibly startled by my appearance. Her concern was palpable as she inquired about my well-being.

Upon seeing me, Professor Olomola's face contorted with shock and sorrow. "Why are you crying, Dare? Is everything alright?" he inquired, his voice filled with apprehension. I could no longer suppress the truth. "Boda Gbenga has passed away," I uttered, my voice barely audible. His response was immediate and heartfelt, "How is my friend?" he asked, referring to my father. I confessed my uncertainty, explaining that I sought his wisdom to navigate this painful task.

With a heavy sigh and teary eyes, Professor Olomola offered solace. "Go home, Dare," he advised. "Rest, and meet me on campus tomorrow morning at seven." As I departed, I carried the weight of grief and the daunting responsibility of delivering the devastating news. The night was a harbinger of sorrow, a night etched indelibly into the tapestry of my life.

I masked my grief, feigning normalcy before my father. Surprised by my unexpected visit, he inquired about my reason for coming. I concocted a feeble excuse, I told him I had few things to sort out on campus the next day. I informed him I would be leaving the house early the next day. I left him in the sitting room claiming a headache and a desire for an early night. The ritual of our nightly conversations, a cherished tradition, was shattered. As I retreated to my room, tears streamed down my face. The weight of the impending tragedy, the unbearable burden of delivering the devastating news to my father, consumed me. How would he bear the loss of his beloved son?

The following morning, I met with Professor Olomola, who had coordinated with a pastor from my father's church. Together, they arrived at our home, their somber presence signaling an impending catastrophe. My father, sensing the gravity of the situation, demanded an explanation for their early visit. A mournful silence hung heavy in the air as they delivered the heart-wrenching news. His light, his source of joy, had been extinguished. His anguished cries echoed through the house, a mournful symphony of grief.

I witnessed his despair from the confines of my room, feeling the depth of his sorrow. The weight of the tragedy was overwhelming, and I could only imagine the pain he must have endured. As he learned that I was already aware of Gbenga's passing, he turned to me, his eyes filled with tears. He embraced me, a silent plea for solace. In that moment, I knew I had to be strong, to support him through this darkest hour. I informed him of my intention to travel to Benin, to comfort Gbenga's wife and children. As I prepared to leave, I felt a profound sense of sorrow and responsibility. The future, once filled with promise, now seemed uncertain and bleak.

The weight of delivering the mournful news to my father had lifted, but a new burden pressed upon me. It was time to embark on a journey to Benin, a pilgrimage of sorrow, to offer solace to my brother's bereaved family. Departing from Ile-Ife at midday, I arrived in Benin City around five in the evening. Making my way to my brother's residence at 1 Ogbewe Street, GRA, I was met with a somber atmosphere. The compound was filled with mourners, each offering their condolences to the grieving family.

Upon seeing my younger brother, Tosin, we embraced in a silent communion of grief. He recounted the tragic events, his voice heavy with sorrow. Members of the Redeemed Christian Church, where my brother had served as a pastor, were present, along with representatives from the State Pastorate. Their solidarity offered a measure of comfort to the grieving family.

As I sat in my brother's living room, greeting the mourners, his three young children approached me: Godsmercy, 5; Godslove, 3; and Godsfavour, just over a year old. Too young to comprehend the depth of their loss, they found solace in my presence. Little Godsfavour clung to me, her innocent trust a stark contrast to the somber reality.

Aunty Bola, a woman of quiet strength, was visibly shaken by my arrival. Overwhelmed by grief, she sought solace in my embrace, then she said "there's something I need to tell you," she began, her eyes filled with a mixture of agony and sorrow. "I'm a few months pregnant." A wave of despair washed over me. My heart, once hopeful, now sank into the depths of despair. A question echoed in my mind, a query directed at the heavens: "Why, God, why would You inflict such suffering upon us?" A sense of injustice gnawed at me. My brother, a beacon of kindness and innocence, did not deserve this cruel twist of fate.

Pastor Femi, a man of God and my late brother's pastor at RCCG Ogbewe Quarters, Agbor Park, found me grappling with a profound question of faith. In my anguish, I challenged the divine plan, questioning why my brother, a pillar of strength and a beacon of righteousness, had been taken before others, perhaps even before the General Overseer himself.

Pastor Femi, ever the compassionate guide, turned to the ancient wisdom of scripture. He opened the sacred text to Isaiah 57:1-2, where the prophet pondered the mysterious ways of the Lord. "The righteous perish, the godly die young, and no one seems to care or wonder why. No one seems to understand that the Lord is shielding them from the evil to come. For those who follow godly paths will rest in peace when they die."

In that moment, my heart rebelled against the divine decree. How could such a righteous soul be claimed so soon? But Pastor Femi, with his quiet wisdom, did not offer a simple answer. Instead, he simply acknowledged my pain and offered his prayers for the grieving family.

Through this experience, I learned a valuable lesson: the limits of human understanding. When faced with the inexplicable, it is often best to surrender to the divine will. To question the ways of the Lord is to invite further sorrow. In the face of loss, silence can be a more potent form of solace than words, a testament to the depth of empathy and the power of prayer.

The following day, the weight of grief compelled me to initiate the preparations for my brother's funeral. Before any plans could be made, I felt an urgent need to see him one last time. I visited the University of Benin Teaching Hospital mortuary, armed with a fresh set of clothes to replace the blood-stained garments he wore in his final moments.

As I entered the mortuary, a scene of chilling desolation unfolded before me. A macabre tableau of unclaimed bodies, piled high like discarded refuse, awaited their mass burial. The sight was a sobering reminder of life's fragility and the inevitability of death. I couldn't help but ponder the futility of our earthly pursuits, the ceaseless striving for wealth, power, and recognition, all of which fade into insignificance in the face of mortality.

As I was led into a dimly lit room, I encountered my brother, his lifeless form resting on a cold, metallic platform. In that surreal moment, he appeared to be merely asleep, his peaceful countenance betraying the violent end that had befallen him. I gently called out his name and asked him to wake up, "*Boda Gbenga, e di de*," a plea that echoed through the silent room. My voice, heavy with sorrow, broke the stillness as I wept uncontrollably. The once vibrant and resilient Gbenga, the pillar of our family, had been silenced forever. The elephant had fallen, the warrior had succumbed.

The sight of the deep wound on his head, a testament to the brutal force of the accident, was a harrowing reminder of his violent demise. Despite his indomitable spirit, even he could not conquer the ultimate adversary. As I stood there, mourning the loss of my beloved brother, I was forced to confront the harsh reality of life's impermanence.

On the fateful day, a mere hours before his untimely demise, he reached out to Tayo through his mobile phone, his voice filled with warmth and gratitude. Their conversation flowed, a testament to their enduring bond. He expressed his sincere appreciation for Tayo's unwavering support, particularly for bailing him out of all his debts and providing for the family since his lucrative job at Globacom Nigeria. Their discussion meandered, touching upon future aspirations. He spoke of his plans to acquire land in Ado Ekiti, our ancestral home, and build a new house, a symbol of prosperity and security. He also envisioned a future where our father would be closer, relocating from Ile-Ife to the tranquility of Ado Ekiti.

The weight of funeral arrangements fell upon Tayo's shoulders. Despite the demanding nature of his job, he tirelessly coordinated and financed the proceedings. Though physically distant, his spirit was present, guiding the process and ensuring a dignified farewell for his departed brother. Tayo, with characteristic efficiency, had already secured a plot of land in the serene Onanla area of Oke-Ila Ado Ekiti, facilitated by our late uncle, Pastor Opeyemi Anuodo. Funds were swiftly transferred to prepare the site for the impending burial. While in Benin, I immersed myself in the somber task of selecting a fitting casket, a final resting place befitting my brother's memory. Our family, alongside members of the RCCG Benin community and my brother's colleagues, meticulously planned a memorial service to honor his life.

Days later, my brother's remains were transported to our ancestral home, where a solemn funeral service was conducted under the auspices of the Redeemed Christian Church of God. A procession of mourners, many traveling the arduous five-hour journey from Benin to Ado Ekiti, paid their final respects. As we stood vigil by the casket, a hushed whisper from my cousin, Adeleke Omolade, now a distinguished professor of Economics at Federal University Oye, sent a ripple of unease through my heart.

He informed me that the "*Iyawo ile*", the association of women married into our extended family, had prepared a room within our dilapidated ancestral home, a structure devoid of modern amenities. No electricity, no running water, no modern toilet or bathroom, only a crumbling latrine for my late brother's wife, Auntie Bola, to endure her forty-day mourning period.

In the traditional Yoruba culture, a widow is expected to observe a period of mourning for her deceased husband. The specific customs and rituals vary across different tribes and families. In some cases, the widow is confined to a dark room for forty days, isolated from the outside world and sustained solely by the food and water provided to her. She is forbidden from basking in the sunlight, as she undergoes the prescribed mourning rituals.

Other practices, particularly those rooted in suspicion and superstition, are even more harrowing. In certain communities, the water used to bathe the deceased is administered to the widow, a cruel and archaic belief that implicates her in her husband's untimely demise, whether through witchcraft or other malevolent means. Such practices are a stark reminder of the inhumanity that can persist, even in modern times.

My cousin's words echoed in my ears, a chilling reminder of the archaic practices that still haunted some communities. I vowed to protect my brother's widow from such a fate. Gathering my siblings; Sister Yemisi and my elder brother Tayo, I shared the grim news. Together, we devised a plan to shield her from the clutches of tradition. We would relocate her to Ibadan, to my sister's home in Wakajaiye, where she could find solace and safety.

As soon as the funeral rites were concluded, we acted on our plan. We informed our relatives of our decision, a resolute declaration that left no room for argument. With a sense of purpose, we escorted my brother's wife to her late husband's car and I drove her and the children to Ibadan. In the quiet embrace of Wakajaiye, our sister-in-law and the little children found solace and support.

Five months later, in October 2004, a new life blossomed amidst the grief. A beautiful baby girl was born, a beacon of hope in the darkness. We named her Godsgrace, a testament to the divine intervention that had guided her birth. And in her name, we honored the memory of her father, bestowing upon her the additional name, Oluwagbemiga, a tribute to his late father.

Two decades have passed since my brother departed this mortal world, a vibrant soul extinguished at the tender age of forty. Yet, his spirit endures, etched in the hearts of those he loved. Each day, we cherish the memory of a life well-lived, a testament to his kindness, his humor, and his unwavering faith. As believers, we hold onto the promise of eternal life, confident that we shall reunite with him at the feet of our Lord and Savior, Jesus Christ. Until that blessed day, we cling to the hope of reunion:

Till we meet again, till we meet again,
God be with you till we meet again.
Till we meet at Jesus' feet.
Till we meet again, till we meet again
God be with you till we meet again.

CHAPTER SEVEN
MY CLOSE SHAVE WITH DEATH

My wife was heavily pregnant, with a due date of March 15, 2014. We had already learned from a scan that we were expecting a baby boy. I returned from China to be by her side, eager to welcome our son into the world and offer her the support she needed, especially after the significant disappointment of being denied a visa by the Chinese Embassy in Lagos. Our original plan had been to have our second child in China, just as we had with our first, but fate had other plans for us.

On February 14, 2014, I returned to Nigeria to prepare for our son's arrival. We moved swiftly to ensure the best possible birthing experience for my wife. As staff members of Obafemi Awolowo University, Ile-Ife, we would typically have chosen to deliver at the University Teaching Hospital. However, due to persistent industrial action by the hospital's staff, we devised a Plan B: registering my wife for antenatal care at one of the city's premier private hospitals. This hospital was owned by a renowned gynaecologist who also served as a consultant at the University Teaching Hospital. With both Plan A and Plan B secured, we felt confident and prepared.

On March 17, 2014, our little bundle of joy arrived safely at the Teaching Hospital. In keeping with the time-honoured Yoruba tradition of naming a child on the eighth day, we meticulously planned a fitting ceremony, which took place on March 25, 2014. With the naming ceremony concluded, I turned my attention to the next chapter: completing my postgraduate studies in China.

Unfortunately, my return to China plans coupled with spending some time with my wife and our new baby clashed with my father's 75th birthday celebration. Unable to attend in person, I patiently awaited my son's first post-one month check-up to accompany my wife.

We booked my flight to China for Tuesday, April 22nd, the day after Easter Monday. The day before, my elder brother, Tayo, was returning from our hometown of Ado Ekiti, where he had attended our father's birthday celebration. I asked him to make a brief stopover in Ile-Ife to assist me with my luggage, as I planned to travel by public transport. He obliged, delivered a heart-warming report of the successful birthday event, and continued his journey to Lagos.

The arrival of our new baby necessitated a significant shift in our household dynamics. To lighten the load on my wife, we made the difficult decision to hire a domestic helper. While we had always been wary of strangers in our home, especially those entrusted with the care of our children, the circumstances demanded it. The tales of malevolent house-helps, often wielding supernatural powers to manipulate and ensnare unsuspecting homeowners, were a constant source of worry. Nonetheless, we took a leap of faith, hoping that our vigilance and a touch of luck would safeguard our family. We welcomed Blessing, a young woman from Akwa-Ibom State, into our home.

On Easter Monday, the day before my scheduled departure for China, our church, the Sanctuary of Hope, hosted an Easter celebration with a delicious spread of jollof rice and chicken. We brought our share home to enjoy. As we dined, I noticed that Blessing, our house help, had been given a particularly generous portion of chicken, a succulent piece that dwarfed my own rather bony offering. In a moment of impulsive greed, I swapped our plates. I took the one with the big chicken and left Blessing with the bony one, of course she was not happy but I am the daddy of the house.

However, my act of greed quickly turned sour. As I bit into the juicier piece, one of my molars cracked, sending a jolt of pain through my jaw.

The culprit, it seemed, was a hidden bone fragment. Immediately, I was filled with remorse for my selfish act. A more cynical part of me, however, couldn't shake the suspicion that Blessing might have somehow jinxed the chicken, perhaps using some sort of diabolical power to exact revenge for my earlier transgression.

After dinner, I spent the evening bidding farewell to friends. We visited Professor Bukola Ojo to inform her of my impending departure and caught up with a few other acquaintances. Returning home around 9 PM, I relaxed with my wife and daughter, sharing stories and expressing my love. Finally, around 11 PM, I retired to bed, eager to rest before my long journey.

The clock struck three in the morning, jolting me awake from a nightmarish vision. In the dream, I stood before a sombre coffin, tears streaming down my face. Though the identity of the deceased remained a mystery, the grief was palpable. The dream's impact lingered, manifesting as a searing pain in my abdomen, unlike anything I had ever experienced. Unable to stand, I was plunged into a state of confusion and fear.

My wife, Ajibike, was alarmed by my distress. She recognized the severity of the situation, sensing that this was more than just a simple stomach ache. With a touch of concern, she urged me to rise and pray. In that moment, I realized the spiritual nature of the battle. We began to pace the room, our voices raised in tongues, seeking divine intervention. Suddenly, an urgent need arose. As I rushed to the bathroom, a torrent of watery substance expelled from my body, offering temporary relief. However, upon returning to the living room, my strength waned, and I collapsed. It was clear that we required immediate assistance.

The situation was dire. We were miles from any emergency service, stranded and helpless. Thankfully, my wife, ever resourceful, lifted me into the car and rushed me to the University Clinic's emergency department. The doctor on duty assessed my condition, but it was clear that the matter was beyond their capabilities. Without hesitation, they transferred me to the University Teaching Hospital via ambulance.

Meanwhile, my wife had mobilized our friends through phone calls to provide support. Professor Titilayo, Mr. Oloyede, Dr. Iroju, and

Mr. Dare a namesake of mine had already arrived at the hospital, anxiously awaiting news. She had also alerted Professor Mrs. Faborode, who joined them in the Accident and Emergency Unit of the Teaching Hospital.

At the Accident and Emergency unit of Obafemi Awolowo University Teaching Hospital, It was always a scene of dire distress. A chaotic scene would unfold, marked by shortages of medical personnel and inadequate equipment. Precious time always lost, and patients, teetering on the brink of life and death, were left to suffer.

As expected, the ward was highly overcrowded, with patients spilling out onto the cold, unforgiving floor, their frail bodies hooked to IV drips. The pervasive darkness, a consequence of erratic power supply, cast an eerie glow over the scene. Doctors, armed with feeble flashlights, navigated the gloom, their skilled hands working tirelessly to save lives.

As I was extracted from the ambulance, my weary body was laid unceremoniously upon the cold, bare floor. A stroke of luck intervened when a perceptive unit head recognized my wife and interceded on my behalf, securing a stretcher. There, I lay, a fragile vessel tethered to an IV drip, its saline solution trickling into my veins. For hours, I endured the agony, a solitary figure adrift in a sea of neglect. The promise of a bed seemed as distant as a mirage, and when it finally arrived, it was a cruel jest a space adjacent to an unflushed toilet, its noxious fumes assaulting my senses.

As the hours wore on, a consultant from internal medicine made a cursory examination, misdiagnosing my condition and departing with a dismissive air. A junior doctor, perhaps succumbing to the pressure of an overwhelmed system, was overheard voicing doubts about the severity of my illness, suggesting that I might be exaggerating my symptoms. This callous remark pierced my heart, igniting a silent storm of tears.

For two interminable days, pain and agony were my constant companions. By the third day, my voice was a mere whisper, and a sinister darkness crept into my vision. A wave of nausea overcame me, and I was wracked by violent retching, expelling a substance as black as the void.

As night fell, a harrowing scene unfolded before my eyes. A young man, a victim of a brutal motorcycle accident, was brought into the ward. His body was a canvas of wounds, his lifeblood seeping away. He was laid on a bed adjacent to mine, a stark reminder of the fragility of human existence. Darkness enveloped the room, an oppressive silence broken only by the laboured breaths of the injured man. The doctors, faced with a life-or-death situation, struggled to find his veins in the dim, flickering light of a flashlight. The emergency generator, our lifeline in such dire circumstances, was unavailable for the next two hours.

A desperate plea escaped the man's lips, a haunting echo in the still night. "Please," he begged, his voice barely a whisper, "I don't want to die. My wife has just given birth. I can't leave her." His words, filled with raw desperation, pierced the darkness, a stark reminder of the human cost of neglect and inefficiency. His desperate pleas for life echoed through the sterile ward, a haunting melody of suffering. Yet, as abruptly as it began, his voice faltered, then stilled. A chilling silence enveloped the room, broken only by the rhythmic beep of machines.

I turned to my brother-in-law, Mr. Israel Adeyeye, a seasoned agriculturist and a distinguished figure from the University Farm. His eyes, usually filled with wisdom and kindness, mirrored my own confusion and fear. I stammered, "What happened to him? He couldn't even utter a word, as if his voice was stolen by the very air. "Before he could respond, the bed was wheeled away, the man's form shrouded in a stark white sheet. A hospital staff member, their voice devoid of empathy, confirmed the inevitable: he was gone.

Tears blurred my vision as a wave of grief washed over me. A life, a soul, extinguished with such callous indifference. His final plea, a desperate cry for survival, had been met with the cold, unyielding face of a failing system. It was a stark reminder of the fragility of human life and the cruelty of a world that often turns a blind eye to suffering.

On the third day, Wednesday, a bleak shroud descended upon my spirit. As soon as my wife, Ajibike, arrived, I confessed my fear, my heart heavy with the dread of impending mortality. Hope, a beacon that had guided me through life's storms, had been extinguished. My dreams, once vibrant and boundless, now seemed like fading echoes of a distant past. The gnawing uncertainty within me was a torment that no medical jargon or diagnostic tool could alleviate.

Ajibike, a pillar of strength, refused to let despair consume me. She shared her own burdens, her tireless juggling act between our home and the hospital, a delicate balance disrupted by the arrival of our newborn child. Despite her own trials, she offered unwavering support, reminding me of the resilience of the human spirit. News of my siblings' imminent arrival brought a flicker of comfort, a promise of solidarity in the face of adversity. However, the absence of my children, barred from the emergency ward, cast a long shadow over my heart. I yearned for their innocent faces, their comforting touch, but fate had denied me this simple solace.

As the weight of the previous night's ordeal bore down upon me, the facade of stoic masculinity crumbled. Tears, a silent testament to the depths of my despair, streamed down my face. I was a man undone, a victim of circumstances beyond my control. The sun was high in the sky when my brother, Tayo, arrived from the bustling metropolis of Cotonou. A seasoned legal mind, he held a position of prominence at Globacom Limited. Accompanying him was his esteemed colleague and friend, Pastor Jide. As Tayo's gaze fell upon me, a surge of fraternal love and determination ignited within him. He resolved, with unwavering resolve, to do whatever it took to save my life.

A man of action, Tayo sought the aid of our uncle, Rotimi Kayode, a renowned civil engineer and influential figure in the university community. Rotkay, a man of considerable standing, wasted no time in approaching the Chief Medical Director (CMD). He painted a poignant picture of our family's plight, highlighting the tragic loss of my elder brother and the imminent threat to my own life. Moved by the gravity of the situation, the CMD pledged to intervene. He ordered that the most skilled internal medicine surgeon be assigned to my case.

Professor A.O.Adisa, a renowned Surgeon, was summoned immediately. Unfortunately, he was out of town with his family in Ibadan. Despite the distance, he swiftly made his way to Ile-Ife, driven by a sense of urgency and compassion. Upon examining my condition, Professor Adisa delivered a sobering assessment. He explained that immediate surgical intervention was the only hope for my survival. Time was of the essence; a delay of even an hour could prove fatal.

The theatre entrance was a blur of familiar faces, a sombre tableau of friends, church members, and colleagues from Obafemi Awolowo University. Each offered well wishes, their voices muffled by the weight of my impending ordeal. As I gazed upon them, tears streamed down my face, not merely from physical pain, but from the overwhelming grief of loss. My wife, my children, my siblings, my friends, all were slipping away, leaving an aching void in my heart.

In that moment, life seemed inconsequential. All I yearned for was an escape from the torment, a passage to the eternal embrace of my creator. A spectral procession began to form, a haunting parade of the departed. My mother, long gone, and Brother Gbenga, whose absence had cast a shadow for a decade, materialized before me, their expressions etched with sorrow. They mourned the premature end I sought, their silent pleas echoing in the recesses of my mind.

As the cold, unforgiving metal of the gurney bore me away, I bade a silent farewell to the world I knew. The theatre doors swung shut, sealing my fate and ushering me into the unknown. The sterile operating theatre, a stark, clinical space, was the stage for my impending transformation. A wave of anticipation washed over me as I awaited the anaesthetic's embrace. The anaesthesiologist's voice, a soothing melody, guided me into the abyss as I counted down "Ten, nine, eight, and seven..." and darkness claimed me.

I awoke in a surreal realm, a vast, ethereal hall filled with countless souls, each reclining upon a pristine white bed. A cacophony of voices filled the air, a haunting chorus of lamentations. One voice, a man's, echoed with self-recrimination, confessing his greed as the cause of his untimely demise. Another, a woman's, lamented her sloth, her failure to fight for life. Among these spectral figures, I recognized a face, a victim of a tragic motorcycle accident from the previous day. His spectral form recounted a harrowing tale of medical negligence, a life cut short by a system's indifference.

As I yearned to interject, a disembodied voice silenced me, a stern reminder of my fleeting existence. Fear, a chilling companion, crept into my heart. I yearned for life, yet dreaded the return of the torment that had brought me to this threshold. In that moment, a figure emerged from the shadows, a beacon of hope in the desolate expanse. With a gentle touch, he commanded me to rise, invoking the power of a divine miracle. "Oludare, return to your family!" His voice, a clarion call, shattered the silence.

My eyelids fluttered open, and I found myself enveloped in the warm embrace of reality. The sterile hospital room, a stark contrast to the ethereal realm, was bathed in the soft glow of a single lamp. The face of my nephew, a 15 year old Adeola Adeyeye (now a Computer Engineer), beamed with joy, his voice echoing the words that had awakened me from the precipice of the unknown. "Glory be to God! My uncle has woken up!"

The surgeon, Professor Olawale Adisa, a man of science and precision, our beacon of hope in that tumultuous period, later elucidated to my brother, Tayo, the nature of my affliction: a sigmoid volvulus, a perilous twisting of the intestine demanding immediate surgical intervention. He explained that the prolonged agony I endured was a consequence of the delayed diagnosis, a result of abdominal adhesion, the lingering scars of my 2010 appendectomy performed in China. With a reassuring tone, he assured us of my full recovery. My brother, overwhelmed with gratitude, thanked him for saving my life.

While the medical explanation absolved our house-help of any supernatural involvement, my sister, guided by divine revelation, discerned a deeper, spiritual dimension to my ordeal. A celestial battle was being waged, and spiritual adversaries had targeted our family, their plan was to take another son of my father, on the nose of ten years, after the death of our first born, Gbenga in 2004. Even before the operation, she was comforted by a divine assurance, a promise of victory over the unseen forces that threatened my life.

On the third day, I was discharged, a survivor of both physical and spiritual trials. Reflecting on this ordeal, I recognize the intricate interplay of earthly and heavenly forces. My brother's swift action to leave his work in faraway Cotonou and be physically present coupled with the surgeon's skill were the physical instruments of my salvation. While the fervent prayers of my family and friends were the spiritual armour that shielded me.

As the surgical team worked tirelessly, Ajibike, my guardian angel with a one-month old baby at hand, joined Professor Bukola Ojo in a vigil, somewhere along Ilesha road, Ile-Ife, their prayers intertwining with the medical procedures. Simultaneously, a dedicated group from my church, Sanctuary of Hope, Ile-Ife, mobilized by my wife's friend, Dr. Mrs. Foluke Bamidele formed a prayer chain, their collective supplications echoing through the divine realm. It was perhaps this harmonious blend of earthly and spiritual intervention that compelled an invincible voice to beckon me from the ethereal plane, urging me to return to my family, even as I yearned to linger in that celestial sanctuary.

FROM THE BRINK OF DEATH: A MIRACULOUS SURVIVAL

Earlier on, in the year 2002, during my Youth Corps programme, I embarked on a journey from the rural tranquillity of Umuakagu, nestled within Ehime Mbano Local Government Area of Imo State, where I was fulfilling my national youth service obligation. My destination was the ancient city of Ile-Ife, a pilgrimage of sorts to drive members of my family to Abuja the Federal Capital Territory of Nigeria to witness a momentous occasion. However, my itinerary necessitated a detour to Benin, a bustling metropolis, to visit my eldest brother, Gbenga, a dedicated officer of the Federal Road Safety Corps.

I arrived in Benin around the stroke of nine in the morning, I discovered that broda Gbenga was already engrossed in his daily duties at Agbor Park Federal Road Safety State Headquarter. My nocturnal journey had borne fruit, allowing me to reach the city at such an early hour. Broda Gbenga's joy at my arrival was palpable. He shared his plans to travel from Benin to Abuja to attend the significant event that had brought me to Nigeria. In a mere ten days, Tayo, my elder brother, would be called to the Nigerian Bar, a monumental achievement not only for our family but for our entire kindred. He would be the first to attain the prestigious title of Barrister at Law and Solicitor, a feat that filled us all with immense pride.

The prospect of a son of Michael Afolabi Anuodo becoming the first lawyer in our lineage was a source of immense pride. To honour this momentous occasion, I chose to temporarily suspend my national service duties and join my family in the nation's capital. A month prior, Tayo had undertaken a similar journey, traversing the distance to Umuakagu to inquire about my well-being and to personally extend the invitation to his call to the bar.

Broda Gbenga, the eldest son of my father, greeted me warmly upon my arrival in Benin. After inquiring about my nocturnal journey from Eastern Nigeria, I assured him I had slept through the night. As a seasoned Road Safety Commander, he was deeply concerned about nighttime travel, emphasizing the increased risk and the limited availability of emergency services in Nigeria's rural areas.

He urged me to adjust my travel plans to avoid late-night journeys, suggesting the Benin-Ile-Ife route as a more viable option, despite the deplorable road conditions, particularly the notorious Benin-Ore axis. He insisted on punctuality, emphasizing the importance of leaving early to mitigate the impact of traffic and road hazards.

As usual, Broda Gbenga ordered a hearty meal of rice, beans, and stew, which I devoured eagerly, having fasted since morning. After the meal, he offered to drop me off at the University of Benin Gate, a popular boarding point for buses heading to Lagos and other parts of Southwest Nigeria. Though he insisted on providing me with transport fare, I declined, assuring him I had sufficient funds. Instead, he discreetly placed some money in an envelope, entrusting me to deliver it to our father in Ile-Ife. With a heartfelt prayer, he bid me farewell.

I boarded a Lagos-bound bus, planning to alight at Ore and continue my journey. The arduous journey from Benin to Ore, exacerbated by the poor road conditions and heavy traffic, took nearly three hours. Upon reaching Ore, I joined a 14-seater bus heading to Ile-Ife, securing the last available seat. The bus conductor, a fellow passenger, claimed the space in front of me, perching on the edge of the engine cover with one leg awkwardly positioned between my legs. Despite my towering height, I was forced to endure this uncomfortable arrangement, as no other passenger was willing to relinquish their seat.

As the journey progressed, I yearned for a more comfortable position, hoping that a vacant seat would soon become available. After an hour, a passenger disembarked from the front row, offering a glimmer of hope. However, my aspirations were quickly dashed as the driver, ever opportunistic, had already installed a makeshift seat atop the engine, a notoriously uncomfortable perch. This practice, while increasing the bus's passenger capacity and revenue, prioritized profit over passenger comfort.

As I contemplated my options, I realized that I was not alone in my discomfort. The man seated on the makeshift seat, equally dissatisfied with his own cramped quarters, had his eyes fixed on the same coveted seat. A silent battle for a more comfortable position ensued, a microcosm of the constant struggle for survival and comfort in a world often indifferent to individual needs.

The man alighted, and I rose from my seat, intending to claim the vacant position. However, the passenger occupying the middle seat in the row ahead asserted his right to the coveted window seat, insisting that I should take his less desirable position. I politely declined, explaining that my height would make the middle seat uncomfortable. His response was a surge of indignation, his voice rising as he demanded that I either accept his offer or return to my original seat. The ensuing commotion disrupted the tranquility of the bus, with the majority of passengers siding with the man, arguing that he had a prior claim to the window seat.

The driver, siding with the majority, issued a stark ultimatum: either I complied with their demands or he would refund my fare and force me to disembark. I refused, insisting that he either reverse the bus and return me to Benin or allow me to sit in the front seat. The passengers, exasperated by my stubbornness, derided me as a difficult and unreasonable person.

Despite the mounting pressure, I remained resolute. Finally, the man in the middle seat, recognizing the futility of the conflict, relented and returned to his original position. I gratefully accepted the coveted seat by the door.

As the bus journeyed to Ondo, a mere thirty-minute ride, I succumbed to exhaustion and drifted into sleep. The following day, I awoke to the sight of a young woman, a National Youth Corps volunteer, clad in her official uniform. Her excitement was palpable as she approached me, her simple question, "What is your name?", hanging in the air. I remained unresponsive, my mind still clouded by how I became a patient on a hospital bed. She, sensing my confusion, quickly summoned a doctor.

The physician, a figure of authority and compassion, posed a series of questions, each answered with a clarity born of a fading consciousness. He then revealed a harrowing truth: the bus transporting me from Ore had been involved in a catastrophic accident, claiming the lives of three souls, including the driver.

As bystanders rushed to the scene, I had been mistaken for one of the fallen, left submerged in a pool of my own blood while efforts were directed towards those who still clung to life. A vigilant old woman, however, had noticed bleeding in my wrist, she insisted that if I had died, my heart would no longer be pumping blood, a glimmer of hope amidst the devastation. It was her keen observation that prompted the life-saving intervention.

As the doctor recounted this ordeal, my eldest brother entered the room. Upon seeing me, he erupted in a fervent display of gratitude, rolling on the floor in praise of the divine. He later confided that he had made a solemn vow to God, promising such a gesture if I were to survive. The hospital had contacted him after discovering his complimentary card in my pocket, a lifeline that led them to him.

The man with whom I had that unfortunate altercation over seat succumbed to death two days after the accident as a result of severe spinal injuries he sustained. A heavy weight settled upon my heart, but I knew I could not alter the course of fate. It was not hitherto, my time to die. Yet, amidst the sorrow, a glimmer of hope emerged. I believe that the woman who intervened, urging the rescue team to include me among the wounded rather than the deceased, was a divine emissary. Though I never had the chance to express my gratitude, her selfless act remains etched in my memory.

I spent the following days convalescing in the hospital, gradually regaining my strength. Upon my discharge, I returned to Ile-Ife. Four days later, I embarked on a journey to Abuja, driving my father, his wife, my sister Yemisi, and her husband. Together, we witnessed a historic event that would forever be etched in the annals of time.

CHAPTER EIGHT
JAPA'- AMBITION, DESPERATION, AND THE RELENTLESS PURSUIT OF A BETTER LIFE BEYOND ONE'S HOMELAND.

MY JAPA STORY

The decision to embark on this literary endeavor was a daunting one. It wasn't a lack of material that held me back, but rather a deep-seated reluctance to prematurely frame a story still in progress. This chapter of my life, still unfolding, felt too fluid, too dynamic to be captured in its entirety.

Seeking guidance, I turned to my wife, my unwavering confidante and muse. Sharing my doubts and indecision, I poured my heart out. My younger brother, Femi, also offered words of encouragement, echoing my wife's sentiment. They urged me to document the transformative events that led me to *Japa*, suggesting that upon my return home, I could revisit and review this chapter, incorporating the full spectrum of my "Japa" experience.

And so, I resolved to title this chapter "Japa," a colloquial Nigerian term that has become a cultural touchstone, encapsulating the mass exodus of Nigerians to Western nations, particularly the United Kingdom, the United States, and Canada, in the post-COVID-19 era. It is a word that carries the weight of ambition, desperation, and the relentless pursuit of a better life beyond one's homeland.

The COVID-19 pandemic cast a long shadow over Nigeria, plunging the nation into economic turmoil. As if this global crisis were not enough, the country was further destabilized by the political chaos that ensued during the waning days of the Buhari administration. A toxic brew of corruption, nepotism, and disregard for the rule of law exacerbated the economic downturn, pushing countless Nigerians to the brink of despair.

My wife and I, university professors, found ourselves unexpectedly caught in the undertow of this economic maelstrom. Our once-stable academic careers were reduced to a meager combined monthly income of approximately two hundred pounds (£200), barely enough to sustain our family. The specter of hunger loomed large, forcing us to rely on borrowed funds and supports from family and friends to provide for our needs, most especially those of our children.

In 2016, the Nigerian president infamously labeled the nation's youth as lazy. Little did he know that many of us were quietly striving to survive, even in the face of adversity. As a university lecturer, I had cultivated a small subsistence farm and poultry business in my backyard, supplementing our income with the sale of poultry products. This humble endeavor, born out of necessity, became a lifeline for my family during the darkest hours of the economic crisis.

I expanded my professional horizons into property management and data analysis, consulting for a diverse clientele ranging from individuals to corporations and political entities. Yet, even these additional streams of income proved insufficient to counterbalance the relentless rise in living costs, particularly the exorbitant price of fuel, which made daily commutes and business travel increasingly burdensome.

A shadow fell across my spirit, a subtle disquiet that began to erode the bedrock of my past choices. Had I erred in life's grand equation, miscalculating my course? This question reverberated within me, amplified by the starkness of my present reality. The path of academia, once so alluring, now appeared a perilous divergence from a more promising road—perhaps the bustling highway of commerce, a world I had glimpsed but never truly traversed.

In my youth, the hallowed halls of academia had not beckoned. They were not the object of my ambition, not the destination I envisioned. Yet, fate, or perhaps a confluence of destiny and circumstance, propelled me forward. I found myself scaling academic heights with an unforeseen ease, breaking records, accumulating degrees like precious stones. I became the first Nigerian to achieve the remarkable feat of holding four degrees in Demography and Social Statistics: a BSc, an MSc, an MPhil, and finally, the crowning achievement, a PhD.

This was not a solitary triumph. My wife, a brilliant scholar in her own right, led the way and walked with me on this path. Together, we etched our names into the annals of our family history, becoming the first married couple to both earn doctorates and subsequently teach at the nation's most prestigious university. A testament to our dedication, our intellect, and our shared pursuit of knowledge.

These were achievements that once shimmered with promise, beacons of success illuminating our future. Yet, the cruel irony of our present situation cast a long shadow over these past glories. Despite our academic accolades, despite our dedication to the noble profession of teaching, we found ourselves struggling to provide for our family. The basic necessities of life, the simple act of putting food on the table for ourselves and our two children, had become a daily struggle. A stark contrast to the image of successful academics we once embodied.

The disparity between our perceived status and our actual financial situation became painfully apparent during family gatherings. When the time came to share the financial responsibilities of extended family events, a subtle, yet deeply wounding, exemption was always granted to us. "They are poor lecturers," was the whispered justification, a phrase that stung like a physical blow, a constant reminder of our precarious financial state.

This predicament, this descent into financial hardship despite our intellectual achievements, was not a consequence of personal failings, but rather a reflection of a systemic neglect. The Nigerian government's chronic underfunding of university education had created a climate where academic excellence was rewarded not with material comfort, but with financial insecurity. A pervasive belief, deeply ingrained in the national psyche, held that "the rewards of teachers are in heaven." This sentiment, often expressed with a disarming sincerity, served as a convenient excuse for neglecting the financial well-being of those tasked with shaping the minds of future generations. Another popular, and equally damaging, saying suggested that "if teachers are well paid, they won't concentrate on classroom teaching and impacting knowledge," a notion that effectively pitted financial security against pedagogical dedication.

We had arrived at a crossroads, a critical juncture in our lives. The weight of our circumstances forced us to confront a difficult truth: a reassessment of our life's trajectory was not merely desirable, it was essential. A deep and earnest conversation ensued between my wife and myself, a conversation born of necessity, fueled by a desire to chart a new course, one that would lead us and our children towards a more secure and fulfilling future.

Each morning, save for the Sunday, my wife and I would embark on about ninety-minute walk through the serene confines of the University Staff Quarters, a tranquil oasis within the vast expanse of Obafemi Awolowo University. This ritual, born during the height of the Covid-19 pandemic, provided a much-needed respite from the global turmoil. As the world retreated indoors, we found solace in the gentle rhythm of our daily walks, a solitary communion with nature and the divine.

On this particular morning, as the first blush of dawn painted the sky, I arose, eager to embark on my solitary pilgrimage. My wife, having forewarned me of her absence, I set out alone, anticipating a moment of quiet reflection. The usual cadence of my prayers, a familiar symphony of gratitude and intercession, was interrupted by an unexpected stillness. A divine whisper, soft yet profound, echoed within my soul: "Be still, and know that I am God." The words, both comforting and unsettling, suspended my habitual supplications, inviting me into a deeper, more contemplative silence.

THE AVIAN MESSENGERS: *GBERA* CHORUS

Half an hour into my solitary walk, a peculiar avian chorus began to accompany my steps. A flock of birds, their flight both erratic and purposeful, seemed to shadow my progress. At first, I dismissed this avian escort as a mere quirk of nature, a common occurrence in our verdant, wildlife-rich enclave. Our home, nestled amidst a thicket of dense foliage, had often been likened to a secluded forest by bemused visitors from the bustling metropolis of Lagos.

As the birds' insistent calls, a repetitive "*gbera, gbera*," grew louder, my curiosity turned to unease. Could these feathered messengers be harbingers of impending danger? Perhaps my family, left sleeping peacefully at home, were in peril, and the birds, with their uncanny intuition, were urging me to hasten my return. Overwhelmed by a sudden impulse, I paused my silent meditation and lifted my heart in fervent prayer, seeking divine illumination.

As I neared my residence, a revelation, startling and profound, washed over me. A celestial decree, conveyed through the enigmatic avian chorus, demanded my departure from Nigeria. The Holy Spirit, the interpreter of divine mysteries, had deciphered the cryptic message: *"Gbera"* – a clarion call to abandon my homeland. The destination of this forced exodus remained shrouded in uncertainty, a perplexing enigma yet to be unveiled.

I recounted my extraordinary morning walk to my wife, sharing the divine message conveyed by the avian messengers. We prayed together, seeking further clarity and guidance. As days turned into weeks, my conviction grew stronger. I had concluded that a chapter of my life in Nigeria had drawn to a close, and I must heed the celestial directive to depart. I embarked on a quest to secure a postdoctoral fellowship overseas, submitting applications to universities and institutions in Canada and the United States.

Among the various postdoctoral positions I applied for, one opportunity stood out: the

Postdoctoral Associate position at the Aurora Community Health Commons, University of Colorado Boulder. Before submitting my application, I consulted with esteemed academics to strengthen my candidacy. Professor Sola Asa, a renowned demographer, who supervised my PhD thesis and mentor, penned powerful letters of recommendation. Additionally, Professor Jacob Kehinde Olupona, a distinguished scholar of African and African American Studies at Harvard University, generously offered his guidance and support, leveraging his academic stature to connect me with a prominent American professor who provided expert advice on crafting my application. Despite my confidence, I received the disheartening news that my application had been unsuccessful due to intense competition. The disappointment was profound, but it did not deter my unwavering resolve to leave Nigeria.

Desperate for relocation, I turned to an old friend, Taiwo Adejuwon. We'd shared countless childhood memories and teenage dreams. Now, settled in the United States for nearly two decades, he was a beacon of hope, a bridge to a new world. His guidance on the intricate immigration process was invaluable, offering a roadmap through the labyrinthine bureaucracy.

Yet, as I delved deeper into the possibilities, another option emerged. Deji, a compassionate soul I had met during my time in China, had found a new home in Australia. The allure of the "Land Down Under" was undeniable, a distant dream tempered by the harsh realities of geographical distance and limited opportunities. While Deji's advice was sound, the practicalities of relocating to the Southern Hemisphere proved to be a formidable challenge.

As the world began to emerge from the shadows of the COVID-19 pandemic in the autumn of 2020, a wave of change swept through our church community. Bisi Olaiya, a valued colleague from the security unit at Sanctuary of Hope Church, Ile-Ife, announced his intention to relocate to the United Kingdom with his wife, a skilled psychiatrist.

The news, though unexpected, was received with understanding and well wishes. Soon after, two more members of our security team, Dr. Igie, a seasoned consultant dentist, and Mr. Rufus, a talented computer scientist and co-owner of a prominent Group of Schools in Ile-

Ife, also made the decision to embark on a new chapter in the United Kingdom. Their departures marked a significant shift in the dynamics of my plans, leaving behind a void that would be difficult to fill.

With my aspirations of moving to the US, Canada, or Australia seemingly out of reach, I turned my attention to the United Kingdom. Yet, the path to a new life in the UK presented a formidable challenge, a complex labyrinth of visa regulations and financial hurdles. It seemed the most expensive of the options, with limited career prospects to boot.

Undeterred, I sought counsel from friends who had already made the leap, particularly Akeem Adewolu, affectionately known as AKAY. He assured me that the UK, with its rich history and vibrant culture, could indeed provide a fulfilling future for my family. I engaged in a lengthy conversation with Remi Akinsanya, a seasoned logistics expert who had called Scotland home for over fifteen years. He painted a vivid picture of the United Kingdom, extolling its virtues and promising a wealth of opportunities. Bidemi Awosanya, another long-term resident of Scotland, reinforced Remi's enthusiasm, urging me to seize the moment and make the leap. Their collective endorsement bolstered my resolve. Yet, I sought the wisdom of another trusted friend, Kunle Bamiro, affectionately known as "Sir Kay of London." With unwavering conviction, he issued a direct command: "Pack your bags *ore* (meaning - my friend) and leave Nigeria!"

I sought the counsel of Mr. Dotun, a reputable travel agent with firsthand experience of the UK education system. Having studied in the

UK himself and subsequently becoming an authorized admissions representative for a British university in Africa, he was well-versed in the intricacies of the immigration process. Mr. Dotun explained that the post-Brexit landscape, coupled with the ongoing impact of the COVID-19 pandemic, had significantly altered the UK labour market. The government, seeking to address labour shortages, had relaxed visa regulations for postgraduate students, allowing them to bring their families. While this provided a promising avenue, he cautioned that the most financially viable option would be for one of us to pursue a master's degree, enabling the other partner to work full-time to support the family.

The cost implications of such a decision were substantial. Mr. Dotun estimated that, for a family of four, we would need a minimum of

£25,000 to cover tuition fees, flight tickets, and visa expenses. I was dumbfounded by the exorbitant sum required. How could we possibly amass £25,000 with our meager combined income of less than £300 a month? The task seemed insurmountable, a mountain too high to climb. Yet, a flicker of hope ignited within me. I recalled the peculiar incident with the birds, their insistent "*gbera*," a divine nudge to leave the country. This divine intervention, coupled with unwavering faith, calmed my anxious heart.

I assured Mr. Dotun that we would discuss the matter and respond. Together, my wife and I poured our hearts out in prayer, our confidence growing with each passing moment. Despite having earned her PhD a decade earlier, my wife, ever the ambitious scholar, agreed to pursue a Master's degree in a field related to her psychology expertise. This would provide me with the opportunity to work and support our family, as Mr. Dotun had suggested.

With renewed determination, we embarked on a strategic plan to raise the necessary funds. We decided to sell our prized property in Ile-Ife, a promising investment comprising a ten-room hostel and a three-bedroom apartment, situated on two prime plots of land. The strategic location and the potential for future development allowed us to secure a favorable price. We liquidated our assets, leaving no stone unturned. Additionally, we sought financial assistance from the University Cooperative Society and received a substantial loan. A generous family friend from abroad extended a lifeline, offering a loan of £10,000. With each step, the dream seemed to inch closer to reality.

THE LONG FLIGHT TO A NEW LIFE

On that fateful 30th of January, 2022, we bid adieu to the verdant shores of Nigeria. As I reclined within the confines of the Qatar Airways aircraft, my mind was a tempestuous sea, tossed between reflections of our journey and apprehensions about the uncertain future that lay ahead. In stark contrast, my children, Ooreofe and Obafemi, were exuberant, their spirits soaring as they anticipated the brighter prospects that the United Kingdom promised.

Obafemi, a budding football prodigy, yearned to realize his dream of gracing the hallowed turf as a professional footballer. His incessant queries filled the cabin: "Daddy, can I start playing football immediately upon our arrival in the UK?" "Do you think I'll become a star footballer, Daddy?" "How many more hours until we reach our destination?" While I endeavored to answer his questions, some remained unanswered, knowing full well that his curiosity would prompt him to inquire again. Ooreofe, my more composed daughter, observed her surroundings with a serene maturity. Her questions, though fewer, were equally insightful. Both children relished the in-flight amenities, indulging in the delectable cuisine and captivating entertainment.

Our journey was far from direct. A lengthy eight-hour stopover in Doha preceded our final flight to London. The arduous twenty-three-hour odyssey, including the layover, tested our endurance. While we yearned for the convenience of a six-hour British Airways flight from Lagos, the exorbitant cost rendered it unattainable. Every penny was precious, as we were acutely aware of the substantial financial challenges that awaited us. Finally, on the thirty-first of January, 2022, at the stroke of six in the morning, our aircraft touched down at Heathrow Airport's Terminal 5. A collective sigh of relief escaped our lips as we thanked the Almighty for our safe arrival. United Kingdom, here we come!

Having meticulously researched our prospects before our departure from Nigeria, we anticipated a smoother transition to our new life. However, the initial phase proved to be a period of adjustment and unforeseen challenges. Driven by necessity, we sought temporary refuge with Mrs. Soyebo, a cherished family friend and fellow congregant from our church in Nigeria, who graciously offered us her hospitality. After a three-week sojourn under her benevolent roof, we ventured forth, securing our first rented abode. The financial burden was substantial, a hefty sum of 6,500 pounds demanded for a mere three months of occupancy, encompassing both rent and deposit.

A yearning for greater comfort and a more affordable living situation spurred our relocation in June. By July, we had secured a more suitable dwelling in Newport, a move that offered a measure of respite from the initial financial strain. The initial two months were a period of lean subsistence, marked by a precarious financial situation.

Job prospects remained elusive throughout February and March, a period dedicated to intensive professional development. I immersed myself in rigorous training programs, culminating in coveted certifications as a qualified Door Supervisor, CCTV expert, and VIP Protector. Concurrently, I successfully completed my teaching qualifications, enabling me to pursue a career in education across England, Wales, and Scotland.

Clutching my newly acquired credentials, a tangible symbol of my fresh start, I embarked on a grueling thirteen-hour pilgrimage north, a road trip that stretched from the heart of England to the rugged landscapes of Scotland. My heart thrummed with anticipation, eager to reconnect with cherished friends and share the news of my arrival on British shores. My destination: the welcoming haven of Remi's home, the same Remi, a dear friend from our university days, whose encouraging words had been instrumental in my decision to relocate.

The warmth of their greeting, from Remi and his gracious wife, Tosin, was a balm to my weary soul. It was more than a welcome; it was an embrace, a reaffirmation of the bonds of friendship that time and distance had failed to diminish. The joy of reunion was amplified by the serendipitous presence of Toyin Ogunleye, another beloved friend from our university years, who had journeyed from Canada to spend her holiday in Scotland, hosted by Remi. The house buzzed with laughter and the joyful clamor of familiar voices. Tosin, our ever-generous hostess, whom I hadn't seen since their wedding day back in 2008, orchestrated a culinary symphony, a feast that was as much a celebration of our reunion as it was a testament to her culinary prowess. Each dish, a carefully crafted masterpiece, cemented the warmth and depth of our renewed connection.

The following day brought the final piece of our cherished circle into place: Bidemi Awosanya, another treasured classmate, arrived, completing the quartet of friends. The ensuing hours were a precious exchange, a tapestry woven with threads of shared memories, heartfelt laughter, and invaluable wisdom. Our conversations, deep and meaningful, explored the intricacies of life in the UK. A common theme resonated through our discussions: the unwavering truth that perseverance and unwavering dedication were the twin pillars upon which success in this new land was built. My friends, with open hearts and honest voices, shared their own stories of early struggles and eventual triumphs, offering their experiences not as cautionary tales, but as beacons of hope and inspiration. They urged me to embrace the myriad opportunities that this vibrant nation offered, to seize each chance with both hands.

As the time for my departure loomed, a bittersweet undercurrent ran through our conversations. Tosin, with her characteristic generosity and a heart overflowing with kindness, insisted that I forgo the arduous thirteen-hour road journey back to Cardiff. She deemed it an unnecessary hardship, a trial I needn't endure. And then, with a gesture of extraordinary kindness, Tosin and Remi presented me with a gift: a flight ticket from Edinburgh to Cardiff. Words could barely express the depth of my gratitude for their selfless act of love and care. The subsequent flight, a mere fifty-minute hop across the landscape, felt like a gift of time, leaving me refreshed and invigorated, ready to face the challenges and embrace the opportunities that lay ahead in my new life.

Returning to my family in Cardiff, a new chapter unfolded with the dawn of April 1st, 2022. Two months of enforced idleness had weighed heavily, but fortune, it seemed, had finally decided to smile. I secured a position as a mathematics teacher at a local high school, a role that offered a gratifying salary. My certification as a private security operative, a qualification I had wisely pursued, also proved invaluable, opening doors to a steady stream of security assignments in diverse settings.

A rigorous rhythm soon defined my days. From nine in the morning until three in the afternoon, I immersed myself in the world of equations and theorems, guiding young minds through the intricacies of mathematics. A brief two-hour respite followed, a fleeting interlude before I transitioned into my nocturnal role. At six in the evening, I would don the uniform of a security guard, a vigil that would last until the first light of dawn. This became my unwavering routine, a relentless cycle of teaching and guarding. My children, Ooreofe and Obafemi, became accustomed to my absence, their father a figure seen mostly in hurried glimpses. Yet, the steady influx of income brought a tangible sense of relief, a balm to the anxieties that had plagued us.

Slowly, almost imperceptibly at first, the tide began to turn. My employment prospects flourished, bearing fruit that allowed us to systematically chip away at the mountain of debt accumulated during our relocation. The burden of my wife's outstanding tuition fees, a constant source of worry, was finally lifted as we made the full payment. This milestone marked a significant turning point, a symbol of our growing stability. Emboldened by our improving circumstances, we made the decision to relocate to a more spacious and suitable house in Newport, a move that promised a more comfortable and settled life for our family. The sacrifices, the long hours, the fleeting moments with my children all seemed to find their justification in this burgeoning sense of security and the promise of a brighter future.

Meanwhile, Obafemi, driven by an insatiable passion for football, seamlessly integrated into a local children's football club and adapted effortlessly to his new academic environment. Ooreofe, however, encountered initial challenges in adjusting to her unfamiliar surroundings. The absence of her long-time companions cast a shadow over her spirits. We steadfastly encouraged and supported her, guiding her through the complexities of acclimatizing to British life.

While my own transition was not entirely devoid of obstacles, I maintained a resolute focus on the overarching objective. I had entered this new chapter with eyes wide open, fully cognizant of the sacrifices required to forge a fresh beginning in the United Kingdom. As such, I was able to weather life's inevitable storms with equanimity, viewing them as mere trials to be endured in the pursuit of my goals.

The catalyst for my endeavor was the aspiration to provide my children with a brighter future. I am imbued with unwavering confidence in their potential. Having emerged from the crucible of a developing nation and carved a niche for myself on the global stage, I instilled in them the belief that they are destined for greatness. If a humble boy from Ado Ekiti, Southwestern Nigeria could ascend to the hallowed halls of British academia, educating its native students, then the sky is truly the limit for my children.

A NEW CHAPTER

After an arduous six months, juggling the demands of two demanding roles – a high school mathematics teacher and a private security officer – I found myself at a crossroads. A trusted friend, a London-based lawyer, offered sage advice: to secure my future in the UK, I needed to transition from a dependent student visa to a skilled worker visa. She emphasized the importance of seeking employment in sectors listed as experiencing skill shortages.

Intrigued by this suggestion, I embarked on a quest to identify suitable career paths that would not only provide me with a livelihood but also allow me to contribute meaningfully to society. My lifelong fascination with the noble work of the NHS, its unwavering commitment to providing quality healthcare to all, ignited a desire to contribute to this vital institution. I diligently pursued relevant certifications, determined to equip myself with the necessary skills and knowledge to secure a fulfilling role within this esteemed organization. My innate academic aptitude facilitated this endeavor, enabling me to amass a collection of impressive credentials with relative ease.

Armed with these qualifications, I confidently applied for a position at NHS England and was, to my delight, offered a role that I continue to hold with immense pride. This new role has opened up a world of possibilities. Inspired by this newfound vocation, I have set my sights on a future as a registered mental health nurse. With unwavering determination, I am actively pursuing this ambitious goal, confident that it will soon become a reality.

A NEW DAWN

Working with NHS England, I encountered a diverse fabric of fellow Nigerians, each a authentication to the relentless pursuit of a better life. Economic refugees, like myself, we had shed the opulent cloaks of our former positions and status, now united by a common goal. I shared corridors with ex-bank managers, seasoned administrators, and individuals of immense influence, all humbled by the exigencies of their new reality. It was a sobering realization that the hierarchical distinctions of our homeland held little sway in this foreign land.

The elusive dream of a comfortable existence here was inextricably linked to financial stability. A decent living standard necessitated a steady income, sufficient to meet the demands of exorbitant bills and a burgeoning cost of living. When Nigerians abroad reminisce about our homeland, a palpable sense of relief often permeates our discourse. Many of us who had felt stifled by the limitations of their former lives now flourished in this newfound freedom.

While challenges undoubtedly persist, the fundamental security of life and property, coupled with the reliability of essential services, offers a stark contrast to the uncertainties of our past. The promise of regular income, unburdened by bureaucratic delays, and the opportunity to save a portion of one's earnings, provides a sense of financial security that was once a distant dream.

A GUNNER'S DREAM REALIZED

A quarter-century ago, in the year 1999, my heart was captured by the iconic figure of Kanu Nwankwo. Inspired by my compatriot's exploits at Arsenal Football Club, a fervent allegiance was forged. Though financial constraints precluded the acquisition of authentic merchandise, the spirit of fandom was undeterred. A collection of counterfeit jerseys served as a testament to my unwavering support.

Now, residing in the United Kingdom, I had the privilege of sharing this passion with my children. A promise was made: a pilgrimage to the hallowed grounds of the Emirates Stadium. The anticipation was palpable, shared not only by my children but also by my wife, a passive admirer of the club. The day arrived, and we embarked on a two-hour train journey to the heart of North London. The Emirates Stadium welcomed us with open arms, offering an immersive experience. We traversed the players' dressing room, the manager's office, and the hallowed trophy room.

The highlight, however, was the opportunity to lift the invincible trophy of 2003/2004, a moment of pure ecstasy. To touch the same silverware that had been lifted by the likes of Henry, Wenger, Vieira, Bergkamp, and Kanu was a dream come true. Our footballing adventure continued with a live match against Bayern Munich, a team renowned for their unbeaten streak. Arsenal's resounding victory was a testament to the club's enduring legacy.

Beyond the sheer exhilaration of guiding my family through the hallowed halls of the Emirates Stadium, beyond even the electric charge of ninety minutes spent beneath its thunderous stands, a privilege that granted us fleeting glimpses of footballing deities like Saka, Jesus, Martinelli, Saliba, Ødegaard, and Smith Rowe.

I have striven to weave a tapestry of unforgettable holiday experiences for my loved ones. Each summer, my wife and I would carefully synchronize our annual leave, embarking with our children on journeys of discovery. We have immersed ourselves in the vibrant pulse of cities: Glasgow, with its imposing architecture whispering tales of centuries past; Manchester, a crucible forged in the fires of industry and now brimming with cultural energy; and Southampton, a historic gateway to the world's oceans, its docks a testament to maritime ambition.

Our explorations extended beyond the urban sprawl, embracing the picturesque allure of coastal towns: Carlisle, its ancient stones echoing with the footsteps of Roman legions and medieval knights; Portsmouth, a naval bastion steeped in stories of maritime glory, the ghosts of admirals seeming to linger in the sea air; and Barry Island, a haven of nostalgic charm, its golden sands and vibrant amusement arcades evoking the carefree spirit of summers past. A ferry journey across the Solent to the Isle of Wight added a touch of maritime romance, the salty tang of the sea air and the cries of gulls a welcome symphony against the mainland's hum.

These carefully curated excursions are far more than mere holidays; they are sacred interludes, opportunities to shed the weight of everyday life, to replenish our weary spirits, and, most importantly, to fortify the enduring bonds that bind us as a family. They are chapters etched in shared laughter echoing across windswept beaches, in whispered secrets carried on the sea breeze, and in the quiet contentment of simply being present with one another, creating memories that will endure long after the sun-kissed skin has faded and the suitcases have been relegated to the attic's dusty embrace.

As I prefaced this chapter, recounting this particular juncture of my life has proven a delicate undertaking, for its narrative remains in flux, a story still being written. However, I am indebted to the counsel of those who urged me to chronicle the impetus, the circumstances, and the very mechanics of my departure from Nigeria for the United Kingdom. Hindsight, as I approach the third anniversary of my arrival on these shores, confirms the rectitude of that pivotal decision. I harbor no regrets for exchanging the familiar landscapes of my homeland for the opportunities that have unfolded here.

I am convinced of the value I can contribute to this nation, a nation already steeped in history and achievement. Though my contributions have thus far been modest, I possess an unwavering confidence in my capacity to make a more substantial impact in the years to come. While my earnings here in the UK, though comfortably above average, might not represent vast riches, they have enabled me to provide a secure and joyful life for my family. My children, the very essence of my pride, are flourishing academically and excelling in their chosen extracurricular pursuits.

These past three years have also allowed me to extend a helping hand to those back home. I have been able to provide for the needs of my family in Nigeria and offer more substantial support to my siblings. Furthermore, I have actively engaged in philanthropic endeavors within my community, endeavors that bring me profound satisfaction. As I pen these words, just four days before Christmas of 2024, I am sponsoring a ceremony to honor three exceptional teachers from my alma mater, Aquinas College Akure. Numerous young minds have also benefited from scholarship programs I have established, providing them with opportunities that might otherwise have remained beyond their reach. Achievements that once seemed unattainable within the confines of my native land have now become tangible realities.

Reflecting on my decision to "*japa*" – to embark on this journey abroad – I can only offer heartfelt gratitude to God. I acknowledge the guiding hand of Providence, the "avian messengers," who directed me towards this path. To God be the glory.